When
Momma
Died

A Journey to Self

Sherita Moon Seawright

PRESS

ACW Press
Phoenix, Arizona 85013

When Momma Died—A Journey to Self
Copyright ©2001 Sherita Moon Seawright
All rights reserved

Cover design by Alpha Advertising
Interior design by Pine Hill Graphics

Packaged by ACW Press
5501 N. 7th Ave., #502
Phoenix, Arizona 85013
www.acwpress.com
The views expressed or implied in this work do not necessarily reflect those of ACW Press. Ultimate design, content, and editorial accuracy of this work is the responsibility of the author(s).

Library of Congress Cataloging-in-Publication Data

Seawright, Sherita Moon
    When momma died : a journey to self / Sherita Moon
Seawright. — 1st. ed.
    p.cm.
    ISBN: 1-892525-47-X

    1. Seawright, Sherita Moon. 2. Death—Religious
aspects—Christianity. 3. Parents—Death—Religious
aspects—Christianity. 4. Moon, Mattie Aurelia Dillard.
5. Adult children—Religious life. 6. Christian
biography. I. Title.

BV4906.S43 2001   248.8'66
                           QBI01-200190

Printed in the United States of America.

This book is dedicated
to the
memory of
Mattie Aurelia Dillard Moon
June 25, 1928 – March 23, 1991

Table of Contents

Acknowledgments

For me, gratitude is a way of life. I thank God for giving me physical and spiritual life and calling me to the ordained ministry. Without Jesus, I would not be alive today. In response to all that Jesus does for me, I try to serve God by serving others.

Mount Moriah Baptist Church in Clinton, South Carolina holds a special place in my heart. It was there that I first heard the Sunday School Superintendent read the words of Psalm 46 from the King James Version of The Holy Bible, "God shall help her, and that right early." At Mount Moriah I accepted Jesus Christ, was baptized, served as the church pianist, and taught my first Sunday school class. Thank you for giving me a strong spiritual foundation.

The Union Bethel African Methodist Episcopal Church family of Brandywine, Maryland, weathered the storms of my transition from Missionary Society President to Minister to Assistant Pastor. The Ministerial Staff is extremely loving and supportive. Being with you helps increase my faith in God.

The Community Ministry of Prince George's County (Maryland) family helped me learn to live in the faith that God is my source.

I am grateful to all the pastors, preachers, and their spouses and widows, churches, women's and men's groups, and civic and social organizations for your encouragement.

Several people read the manuscript and provided honest, and sometimes painful, editorial assistance: Kimberly (Hazel) Jones, Sonji Reynolds, Bernice Sanders Smoot, Syleste Walker, and my cousin Guynell Williams. Thanks to Marlon Woodford for your artistic ideas.

God's timing and plan for my life have proven to be perfect. By following God's leading I was blessed with assistance from

Caroline Smith, Norma Trax (my very good friend), Adele Pogue, and Margaret Keane.

Thank you, Doris Porter, for the words you shared with me in the very early stage of my unacknowledged grief. You gave me hope that I could live again.

I praise God for my relatives, play relatives, and friends in South Carolina and other places.

A special group of ladies nurture my spirit. I thank God for you: Naomi Carter, Gloria Cooper, Matelon Cummings, Melba Evans, Arie Gray, my cousin Brenda Holland, Constance McMorris, and Sisters in Serenity.

God blessed me by giving me in-laws to be my extended family. Thank you for caring about me.

My three aunts continue to love me, each in her own special way: Bannah Moon Adams, Vinnie Moon Blount, and Norma Josephine Dillard Oliver.

I am blessed that my father and stepmother, Peter and Ivy Moon, have allowed me to have a place in their life.

God blessed me to grow up with one brother: Bill (Peter Moon, Jr.) and two sisters: Lovancie Moon and Laurethia Cleveland. I love you, and I'm glad that we are united by blood. We will never succeed in running away from each other forever.

My daringly ambitious daughter, Shari Nicole, and adventurously creative son, Harry Matthew, occupy a very special place of love in my heart. As a part of me, you reflect family traits. As individuals you exemplify the wonders of God who blessed me to be your mother.

Since I never thought I'd get married, I never expected to meet any man as great as my husband, Harry. God brought us together, and I am the recipient of a love that endures. Your tenderness strengthens me, and I pray that God will allow us to continue to grow together in love and in ministry. Thank you for your support of this project and many others. I love you dearly.

In the year that King Uzziah died,
I saw the Lord sitting on a throne,
high and lifted up,
and the train of His robe filled the temple.
Above it stood seraphim;
each one had six wings:
with two he covered his face,
with two he covered his feet,
and with two he flew.

And one cried to another and said:
"Holy, holy, holy is the LORD of host;
The whole earth is full of His glory!"
And the posts of the door were shaken
by the voice of him who cried out,
and the house was filled with smoke.

So I said: "Woe is me, for I am undone!
Because I am a man of unclean lips,
And I dwell in the midst of a people of unclean lips;
For my eyes have seen the king,
The LORD of hosts."

Isaiah 6:1-5

Preface

Have you ever lost a close relative or friend through death? If you are like most people who encounter the living side of death, your life is changed forever. If you are a spiritual person, in the midst of such trauma, your spiritual sisters and brothers probably told you to "Hold onto your faith!" and "Trust God!" But, in the midst of trying to follow this sound advice, your soul was stretched to perform for the public while, in private, it lay prostrate.

When death visits our circle of family and friends, we often feel betrayed. Yet, as spiritual people, especially as Christians, we are practically forbidden by well-meaning Christians to exhibit any emotion that conveys a lack of faith or trust. It is the conflict between our humanity and spirituality that can make us fall apart in the hours of darkness and pain.

Why must Christians choose the way of the strong upper lip? Don't we have the right to experience life without being told that we are being untrue to our faith? Isn't the Holy Spirit our Comforter? Is yielding to the Holy Spirit's comfort a spiritual crime? What's wrong with crying when someone dies? Doesn't crying help Christians live as survivors?

As a person who knows Jesus Christ as Savior and Lord, when my mother died, I suffered tremendously while trying to avoid the side effects of her death. I tried the position of not-grieving-as-those-who-have-no-hope. I tried the I-shall-not-be-moved position. My friends told me that I should rejoice in knowing that Momma had gone to live with God. Since many of their mothers were still alive, I resented their boldness. My birth family fell apart. Nothing made sense. And I was angry with God.

Being in ministry and dealing with people who face death, I know that my experience was not unique. I hope this book will help others to understand that death cannot be ignored by us or logically reasoned for us. My desire is that other people's lives will be blessed by showing how one Christian dealt with the pains of death. This is not an official grieving handbook that's been endorsed by an august body of authorities. Rather, it is a kinship experience, shared so that you, whether as a Christian or non-Christian, can fully know that you can acknowledge your grief experience and still make it to a better day.

You have to do what *you* have to do to get through the going through. You can't rush the process. Only God and time will allow you to heal. It is only then that you can go on and live without pain similar to what I experienced and what I brought upon myself when Momma died.

I don't want to limit this to a book about grief. I gratefully accept the challenge of making this a book for the living to use as we live. Death will come, but as we await the transformation, let's live. I hope this book will give you a different way of looking at life and death. I hope you will be determined to live to the fullest. Remember, on this side of Glory, we live only for a short while.

And So...It Was

Do you remember "the year"? Not the year you were born or married or finished college. Not the year of your first date. "The year" was the time when something happened in your life that was so dramatic that you were transformed forever. You began to see life for what is, a journey. All of the signs indicated that business as usual was no more, and from that point until you died, everything would be different.

Nineteen ninety-one was "the year" for me. I will never forget it. The changes, the pain, and the agony almost killed me. My world turned inside out and upside down. I never imagined the event, and I certainly never thought about the surrounding circumstances, but in 1991, they all came to be.

At 8:50 A.M., Saturday, March 23, 1991, my mother died. Mattie Aurelia Dillard Moon finished her journey through this earthly life. The journey ended in a losing battle with carcinoma of the colon with liver metastasis—colon cancer that had spread to the liver. Momma lived only one month and five days after the diagnosis.

Momma was born on June 25, 1928, in Clinton, South Carolina. Her mother, Laura Dillard Young (Granny), was not married to Momma's biological father. Momma was the sixth child—one child died as an infant—and the third girl.

Momma lived an exciting life. She attended the local school for Colored children and graduated from Bell Street High School. Her higher education began at Coulter Junior College in Cheraw, South Carolina. She studied teaching at Benedict College in Columbia where she graduated in 1957 with a degree in education.

For thirty-four years, she taught in South Carolina at Bethel School in Cross Hill, Midway Elementary School in Mountville, and Clinton Elementary School in Clinton. Teaching was Momma's calling. She embraced the years with intensity and love, experiencing the joys and sorrows of the profession. As a first grade teacher, she found joy in seeing children write their names for the first time and, in some cases, learn their legal name versus a nickname.

In 1946, Aurelia Dillard married Willie Ullysee Peter Moon, the youngest son of a reputable local family. In 1953, their first child was born, the only son and my father's namesake. We call him Bill. Five years later, in 1958, I was born and named Sherita Gayle. The second daughter, Lovancie Valene made her entrance almost three years later in 1961. After a miscarriage, the family was completed in 1967 with the birth of a girl, Laurethia Ann. Momma often bragged to us about why she married Peter Moon. He wanted something in life; hence her children would have a daddy and a better chance in life than she did.

My birth family suffered no real shortage of things. Daddy was always interested in showing or giving us the latest gadgets, and all of us gained a love of cameras from him. Momma and her family (Loveas, Lucile, Iola, and Josephine) were always there for us and played a major positive role in our early lives. And later, there was another brother, William, whom I met in 1967, a few months before Granny died. Daddy's siblings (Bannah, Columbus, and Vinnie) were a part of our world too.

Momma and I had a special kind of relationship. We got along well with each other, but there also seemed to be a strain. Maybe the birth order of my being the oldest girl, or my consistent love of school, or my being prone to clumsiness that ended with my suffering three broken bones and many dislocations and sprains caused the distance between us. Whatever the cause, Momma and I enjoyed each other tremendously. Even in our misunderstandings, we both knew that there was nothing that we wouldn't attempt to help the other. That was a blessing.

November 1978 marked the beginning of the chain of events that eventually would take my mother's life. Momma began to experience abdominal discomfort after eating. I never would have believed those symptoms were the beginning of the end. Had I been in charge of Momma's life, many things would have been done differently, but determining the length of her life wasn't my call. So I had to play with the hand that life dealt to me.

Medical exams led to polyps being removed and a diagnosis of diverticulitis. A change in diet was the medically prescribed plan of attack. The results were not good. Consequently, Momma had several medical procedures in which inches of her colon were removed. Although the surgeries occurred at six-month intervals, these were not preplanned events. They were used to battle symptoms of inflammation. Yet, the digestive problems continued with bloody bowel movements, pain in the abdomen, intolerance of many foods, and an overall sick feeling. Momma didn't complain, but when teaching became a chore for her, we knew trouble lay ahead.

While in graduate school at The Ohio State University, I came home for a term break. Finding no one at home, I inquired of neighbors who told me that Momma had gone to school to clean out her classroom. I rode my bicycle to Clinton Elementary and learned that medical disability had been granted. Momma was retiring. It was 1980 and all of this came as a surprise to me.

Retirement was a major transition for Momma, but, in her usual fashion, she took it in stride. Only one request to tutor was accepted. In this phase of life Momma enjoyed visiting friends, attending church, and spending time with her family.

Daddy retired soon thereafter and their relationship actually began to show signs of the good life. I wondered if this change was the absence of the pressure of being Mrs. Moon's husband, or if, in Daddy's mind, he was no longer living in the shadow of the teacher. Whatever was responsible for this positive change in my parents' relationship, I wanted to find plenty of it, put it in a bottle, and keep it handy for the future.

In September 1983 Momma came to Washington, D.C. to be with my husband, Harry Seawright, and me as we awaited the arrival of our first baby. The due date was September 17, and to make sure she would be present to meet her first GRANDbaby (emphasis hers) she arrived two days earlier. To our surprise, although I was in the early stages of labor, the doctor sent me home with predictions of another two weeks' wait.

Shari Nicole Seawright was born at 7:41 A.M. on Friday, September 16, 1983. Harry and I were excited, but Aurelia Moon was the happiest grandparent on Planet Earth. Momma asked Harry to allow her to use her car to give her first GRANDbaby her first ride home. This put the icing on Momma's cake of grandmotherly ecstasy.

We enjoyed a wonderful week, but on the following Friday Momma mentioned not feeling well. She was weak and unable to move around much. We were baffled by this sudden turn of events. Then, out of desperation for relief, Momma showed us a knot on the side of her hip that was about the size of her fist. We knew that something was terribly wrong.

The next day, barely able to get into the car to go to the airport, Momma returned to South Carolina. She immediately went to bed. A visit to the doctor on Monday revealed that Momma's intestines had ruptured and feces were being deposited into her side, just at her hip, the location of the knot.

After at least one week of draining the area, Momma was diagnosed with Crohn's disease. A colostomy bag was installed. Momma hated it, and was very self-conscious at first, but she had another lease on life. The incision healed, and Momma began to adjust. She often traveled to see her GRANDbaby. When her first grandson was born in 1987, she made her way to Maryland and greeted Harry Matthew Seawright on Sunday, January 11.

The visits to Maryland continued. The GRANDchildren's summers in South Carolina were sprinkled with stays at the grandparents in Clinton and Swansea. Momma participated enthusiastically in all of her children and grandchildren's lives.

On August 27, 1990, Momma and Daddy celebrated forty-four years of marriage. In November of the same year Momma slowed dramatically. She mentioned feeling tired, and the abdominal discomfort returned. December brought a twenty-pound weight loss within a two-week period. My plans to spend Christmas at home in Maryland were changed when my youngest sister (who was in college) told me that coming to South Carolina for the holidays would be in my best interest.

Christmas Day was special. We spent time opening gifts and laughing. That evening Harry, Shari, and Matthew went to visit my in-laws in Swansea. I stayed in Clinton to take Momma to the doctor the next day.

The day after Christmas began early. The first stop was at the gynecologist's office in Greenwood. This follow-up visit brought the news of a spot in one of Momma's breasts "that needed to be taken care of." Momma didn't ask questions, but I did so until Momma told me to calm down and be quiet.

The next stop was more depressing. The doctor was not happy with what Momma told him and instructed her to stay in touch with him about her condition. He gave her a list of prohibited foods. But there was no major cause for alarm. We believed that the Crohn's disease was simply being temporarily active as it had been so many times before.

Upon my return home to Maryland, the frequent calls to and from South Carolina kept me abreast of Momma's medical condition. Laurethia was in her senior year of college, but most of her free time was spent helping Bill and our Aunt Ceal take care of Momma. This bout with Crohn's was different. The conversations with Momma and the reports from my siblings told of weakness and a general uneasiness.

Momma finally made another doctor's appointment in February. As a result, she was immediately admitted to Self Memorial Hospital in Greenwood, South Carolina. More tests were administered. Momma was told that a cancer screening would be done, and the results would be back after 4:00 P.M. Monday.

After the longest weekend I'd experienced in years, I called Momma after 4:30 P.M. Monday. We exchanged pleasantries and then she said calmly, "Well, it's cancer." My heart sank. I felt weak. I gave the phone to Harry, and I cried. The night proved to be long.

Harry and I prepared for the trip to Greenwood. For the most part our arrival at the hospital the following morning was greeted with happiness. Momma was glad to see Harry, Shari, and Matthew. When she saw me the words she spoke tore at my heart. She said, "Where's Lovancie?" In the midst of trying not to cry because of Momma's desire for Lovancie instead of joy at my being there after a ten-hour ride, I mumbled, "Lovancie didn't come."

The entire immediate family and Ceal gathered at the hospital that evening. The air was thick with nervous laughter about good times. Momma told us, "God knows what He's doing, and I'm gonna beat this thing!" We believed her. During all her years of being sick, I don't believe we ever imagined Divine Justice's being so cruel and allowing her to die before Daddy.

The doctor and nurses prepared Momma for chemotherapy. One nurse expressed shock that the sudden and drastic weight loss had been "ignored." She saw that as a clear sign of trouble. The therapeutic plan was five consecutive days of chemotheraphy (starting immediately) and three weeks off. Future treatment would depend upon Momma's physical state. Only the initial series would be administered as an inpatient.

Momma listened carefully to the instructions and precautions. When the nurse warned Momma about waking up in a couple of days with hair on her pillow, Momma told me to bring her wig. Such proactive behavior was unnecessary; her hair grew. The sores that were supposed to have formed in her mouth amounted to one sore that appeared three weeks later. She said, "They kept asking me about it, so I had to get one."

On Monday, March 18, 1991, Momma prepared for the first day of the second series of chemotherapy. After the twenty-eight mile ride to Greenwood, the doctor informed Momma that she was not strong enough for the treatment. In essence he sent her home to die.

My brother called me at work with the news. I called Harry and my Aunt Phine, Momma's sister who lived in Maryland, and Lovancie. I immediately began making plans to go to South Carolina. The next six hours were filled with chaos. Lovancie could not make up her mind, and I didn't want to leave without her. After her third or fourth mental flip-flop, Harry said, "That's it! I'm taking you to the airport!" Bill and Laurethia met me at the Greenville-Spartanburg Airport, and we arrived home late Monday night. I wanted to say "Hi" to Momma, but Laurethia promised me we'd have plenty of time to see her on Tuesday, and in order to make it through the next day, we needed our rest.

The following morning I surprised Momma with my presence. She surprised me by saying, "Sherita, I knew you'd come! Where's Lovancie?" Again I was instantly pained by jealousy. "Lovancie didn't come," I replied.

Lovancie was supposed to be on her way, but experience had taught me not to make promises about relatives. Lovancie called later that morning to tell us that she and her friend were going to another part of South Carolina first, but at our insistence, she made her way directly to Clinton as soon as possible.

Momma was delighted to see Lovancie. A few years had passed since they had been in each other's presence. Lovancie walked into the den, and Momma said, "Lovancie, you finally came!" Getting Momma to her chair that morning had been a true labor of love. But after kissing Lovancie, Momma got up, almost without assistance, and used her walker to get back to her bedroom. She sat on the bed, and *she* lifted her feet onto the bed. She never got out of bed again.

Being the information hound of the family, after taking care of Momma's immediate needs, I called the doctor. I had been in town for more than twelve hours, and I needed facts. The doctor told me that continuing treatment would not be beneficial. Momma's body was shutting down. She would be in a coma in a couple of days and dead by the end of the week. I shared the doctor's report with Daddy and my siblings.

We all reacted in typical Dillard-Moon fashion. Bill began to pace, faster and faster. Lovancie cried, and Laurethia got into her car and left the house. I continued in my be-in-control-and-don't-act-ignorant mode. I'm not sure that I felt anything, but somewhere deep within I think I was hoping against hope. In my opinion the doctor wasn't giving God credit for being in charge. But I wasn't giving up on God.

On Wednesday the Laurens County Hospice made an intake visit. That night, after our activities settled down a little bit, Daddy called a family meeting. We gathered in the den, and an older cousin stayed in the bedroom with Momma. Daddy began with a statement and ended with a question. "Your momma is gonna die. What are we gonna do?" Teary eyes and fear made their presence known. Nobody spoke, but the air was stifled with grief. We looked at each other, and of course, since nobody else was saying anything, I had to talk. My emphatic, logical answer was the obvious, "We're going to have a funeral, and we're going to bury her." With that answer, that I know now was so inappropriate, we went back to whatever we were doing.

Thursday, March 21 really was the final day of our having Momma with us. This was the day she said her goodbyes. It seems that on that day, she found time to talk with all of her children, but only two of us have discussed this. My late Thursday evening chat with her was earth shattering. We talked about old, painful stuff. After our time together I realized that in one sense, I had heard more than I had ever wanted to know, and yet I was relieved to know that I had not been insane for twenty-eight years. She told me to be nice to Harry and my children. When I asked her why she was telling me that, she said, "Because I know you, Sherita."

Shari and Matthew were planning to spend spring break in South Carolina. Momma asked several times about when they were coming. Finally I told her that they weren't coming. She talked with Harry and thanked him "for everything."

Throughout Thursday night Momma talked nonstop. From our strategic location in Laurethia's bedroom, we listened to Momma talk about how she had "lost her house." She told Daddy that "the man from the funeral home came for those other folks and you [Daddy] can go to bed now." She must have known that she was dying.

On Friday morning I prepared the meal that Momma had requested all week: grits (with butter) and toast. Dutifully I took the tray to her bed. She looked at me and said, "I don't want no grits!" I should have known that the end was near. Aurelia Dillard Moon did not use improper English. For two years I couldn't eat grits. My stomach became weak at the thought of placing that food in my mouth.

Friday was the last twenty-four hour period. The colostomy bag that had been attached to catch fecal matter only showed streams of blood. Momma talked of itching and feeling hot inside. The doctor suggested an over-the-counter anti-itch medication. A day earlier I realized that Momma's feet were colder than the rest of her body. My siblings said it was because the fan was blowing directly on her feet. On Friday, the cool feeling was moving up her legs. With my need to know in high gear, I purchased a thermometer and took temperature readings as her body continued to cool.

By Friday night, Lovancie was on her way back home to Washington. Momma was in a fitful state of mind and body. She tossed and turned. She wanted her head to be elevated. As soon as we raised her head, she wanted it lowered. Bill rigged blankets and wooden boards to bring comfort. No matter how we turned her, or tried to do what she said, nothing worked. She just kept talking about her car.

Earlier in the week I told Laurethia that I hoped when we woke up the next morning, it would all be over. That wasn't our

Momma in that bed. That was somebody else who had invaded her body. The Momma we knew and loved wouldn't want people bathing her and helping her with all of her private basic needs. To my statements Laurethia said, "I want one more night." As we climbed into bed that Friday night, Laurethia said, "I don't want any more nights."

Laurethia and I realized that unless a miracle happened, we would need an obituary and funeral program—soon. Since we couldn't sleep, we decided to start right then, not a bit too soon. We finished shortly after 4:00 A.M.; then we slept.

Daddy woke Laurethia and me just before 8:00 A.M. His words were, "I think your momma is dying." We immediately paged Bill. I called Ceal and went to get her. One cousin came from her house across the street, and another cousin, who lived next door, joined us. Daddy's sisters, Aunt Bannah and Aunt Vinnie, arrived quickly.

As we stood around the bed, we were peacefully afraid. Although her mouth was moving, Momma was not talking to any of us. Her eyes seemed to have been rolling aimlessly as she looked toward us. Her shallow breath was punctuated with what I now know to be the "death rattle." I've never forgotten that sound, so distinct, so forceful, so labored, and so real.

Our older cousin, who was familiar with the days when most Black people died at home, told us that because people like to slip away, we needed to leave the room so that Momma could go. As we entered the hallway, Laurethia said, "Momma, I love you." To this, Momma gave her only response of "I love you" to Laurethia. As soon as we left the room our cousin called us back, just in time to see Momma take her last breath.

Standing around the bed, we held hands and prayed, thanking God for allowing Momma to be with us and for receiving her back. We *were* grateful. We knew we had been blessed. At that time nobody was crying; we had things to do. I didn't know then how much my life had changed at the moment of Momma's final breath. But I know now.

Initial Shock

Because God fearfully and wonderfully made all of us individually, God knows that some of the elements of life are best shared with our individual selves bonding with other individual selves. When Momma died, I am convinced that all of her children went into shock. In talking with other persons who have traveled the bereavement trek, my conclusion has become stronger.

Entries from my journal for the week before Momma died let me know that I had prepared for Momma's death more than I knew. My devotional readings and comments:

> *Plans for this week: Go to South Carolina this weekend to check on Momma.*
> *Prayers: for Momma's healing, for strength for my family and me.*
> *Promises: to take better care of myself*

> **Sunday's Scripture-**
> *So Jesus answered and said to them, "Have faith in God. For assuredly, I say to you, whoever says to this mountain, "Be removed and be cast into the sea,' and does not doubt in his heart,*

but believes that those things he says will be done, he will have whatever he says. Therefore, I say to you, whatever things you ask when you pray, believe that you receive them, and you will have them." –Mark 11:22-24

Sunday's Comment- *I am trying to have more faith. Today's worship service was a real struggle for me. I only could think about Momma.*

Monday, Tuesday, and Wednesday's Scriptures-
For I consider that the sufferings of this present time are not worthy to be compared with the glory which shall be revealed in us. For the earnest expectation of the creation eagerly waits for the revealing of the sons of God. For the creation was subjected to futility, not willingly, but because the creation itself also will be delivered from the bondage of corruption into the glorious liberty of the children of God. For we know that the whole creation groans and labors with birth pangs together until now. Not only that, but we also who have the firstfruits of the Spirit, even we ourselves groan within ourselves, eagerly waiting for the adoption, the redemption of our body. For we were saved in this hope, but hope that is seen is not hope; for why does one still hope for what he sees? But if we hope for what we do not see, we eagerly wait for it with perseverance.
Likewise the Spirit also helps in our weaknesses. For we do not know what we should pray for as we ought, but the Spirit Himself makes intercession for us with groanings which cannot be uttered. Now He who searches the hearts knows what the mind of the Spirit is, because He makes intercession for the saints according to the will of God.
And we know that all things work together for good to those who love God, to those who are the called according to His purpose. –Romans 8:18-28

Monday's Comment- *I came to South Carolina. I am confident that God will do his work. I didn't go in Momma's room. I'll wait 'til morning.*

Tuesday's Comment- *I am so glad I came here. Momma looks so different. Her faith is strong. She has no pain. She's very weak. Lovancie came today; I believe Momma was waiting for her. [She] started talking about "the big light."*

Wednesday's Comment- *Momma didn't feel like getting up today. She's still weak. Her appetite is good. She's itching a lot, says her back is on fire. She's all right spiritually. Hospice came today. Her feet are cold. [There was more talk about] the big light. Daddy talked with us tonight.*

Wednesday, Thursday, and Friday's Scriptures-
He who dwells in the secret place of the Most High Shall abide under the shadow of the Almighty. I will say of the LORD, "He is my refuge and my fortress; My God, in Him I will trust."
Surely He shall deliver you from the snare of the fowler And from the perilous pestilence. He shall cover you with His feathers, And under His wings you shall take refuge; His truth shall be your shield and buckler. You shall not be afraid of the terror by night, Nor of the arrow that flies by day, Nor of the pestilence that walks in darkness, Nor of the destruction that lays waste at noonday.
A thousand may fall at your side, And ten thousand at your right hand; But it shall not come near you. Only with your eyes shall you look, And see the reward of the wicked. Because you have made the Lord, who is my refuge, Even the Most High, your dwelling place, No evil shall befall you, Nor shall my plague come near your dwelling; For He shall give His angels charge over you, To keep you in all your ways. In their hands they shall bear you up, Lest you dash your foot against a stone. You shall tread upon the lion and the cobra, The young lion and the serpent you shall trample underfoot.
Because he has set his love upon Me, therefore I will deliver him; I will set him on high, because he has known My name. He shall call upon Me, and I will answer him; I will be with him in trouble; I will deliver him and honor him. With long life I will satisfy him, And show him My salvation. –Psalm 91

Immediately Jesus made His disciples get into the boat and go before Him to the other side, while He sent the multitudes away. And when He had sent the multitudes away, He went up on the mountain by Himself to pray. Now when evening came, He was alone there. —Matthew 14:22, 23

Be merciful to me, O God, for man would swallow me up; Fighting all day he oppresses me. My enemies would hound me all day, For there are many who fight against me, O Most High. Whenever I am afraid, I will trust in You. In God (I will praise His word), In God I have put my trust; I will not fear. What can flesh do to me?... You number my wanderings; Put my tears into Your bottle... —Psalm 56:1-4, 8

Thursday's Comment- Trusting when afraid... Hospice returned with a catheter today. Momma doesn't even know it's there. She is delirious at times. Still no pain. I'm trusting you, God, but I am getting nervous. Every morning I wait to hear Momma's voice. (She lost her house/no water...) [She and I had] a tough conversation.

Friday's Comment- This scripture seems so appropriate today. Momma is failing, but last night she let me know that she is saved. She's not worried. She didn't ask for anything today. I fed her stew meat and rice. She's failing quickly.

Saturday's Scripture-
Man decays like a rotten thing, Like a garment that is moth-eaten. —Job 13:28

Saturday's Comment- Momma passed. I never experienced this before. We were with her. She responded only to Laurethia's statement about love. 8:50 A.M.. I am relieved that she didn't suffer. Everything happened so quickly. I'm alright I think. Cousin _____ is a jewel.

Our initial action after Momma died was to record the time of death, call the hospice nurse, and then the funeral director. As promised, hospice was there in exactly one hour. After taking my mother's vital signs and doing whatever else she had to do, the nurse allowed Laurethia and me to help her prepare Momma for the mortician's arrival. We assisted in putting on the incontinence brief. As I lifted Momma I knew that God would work the miracle right then.

Although an hour had passed, I found myself repeating inside my head, "Okay, God, now's the time! Show yourself! C'mon God!" This mental exercise consumed me, but I took extra care in handling Momma's body. When life returned to her, in what would be only a few minutes, I wanted her not to have been hurt in any way.

I never entertained the remote possibility of the miracle not happening my way. Didn't God promise not to disappoint those who put their trust in Him? Wasn't I trusting God with blind faith? But my miracle never happened. Or did it? Hadn't I released Momma to God? Hadn't all of us, in our own way, given Momma permission to leave us? Yes, we had, and I am convinced that at that time—when we left the room before her final breath—life returned to her. Not in the form for which I had prayed or hoped, but life as all Christians, and probably non-Christians, experience.

Yes, when Momma died we prayed, but we also decided that we wanted pictures of this life-changing time period. After a few photos we ran out of film. Not to fear! Bill and Laurethia went to the store. While they were gone, the funeral director came. When we asked him to wait until we could take more pictures, he must have thought we had lost our minds. He obliged us by asking that we allow him to put Momma on the gurney as he waited.

Armed with a new roll of film, we posed for many pictures. They included pictures of the three children with Daddy, and with our aunts, and just the three of us. We took pictures of Momma's being placed in the hearse, the hearse's leaving the driveway, going down the street, and turning the corner.

When Momma no longer breathed for her family to see, she began to breathe for herself. For the first time in sixty-two years she experienced spiritual breathing, with no congestion; unfettered breathing, free from earthly cares; and deep breathing, filled with the humanly incomprehensible freshness of new life with God.

This level of understanding did not come right away. Many rains would pass before I shook off the cobwebs of archaic spiritual hopes and took on the spiritual realities of life. Coming to grips with the death of a family member takes time. Love or hatred cannot be ignored or forgotten simply because death altered the relationship.

Initial shock is a blessing that grants us time and space to begin tending our interests with an absence of mind that affords us a moment of peace. In this phase of grief we make the necessary and appropriate contacts to get ready to get through the unavoidably present tough time. This absence of mind allows even the best thinker and planner to do what they believe to be is best. This time of dizziness permits the most honest family member to declare to others, "She sure does look good! She looks like she's asleep!"

Initial shock can also be a nightmare. In the hours and days immediately after being faced with death, many families break, sometimes to the point of no return. The funeral preparations take place during initial shock, and failure to list one of the "right" relatives' names in the obituary can bring irrevocable havoc for everybody. Some grief-stricken families experience not speaking to siblings, cousins, or parents because somebody did the unmentionable or unthinkable during what had to be a time when the mind could not possibly function properly.

I am grateful to my mother for preparing us for the financial world of initial shock. The "pay-up-or-shut-up" rule can be, and often is, destroyed during this time. My mother was very clear about funeral arrangements. Her philosophy was plain and simple: "Don't put a whole lot of money in the ground!" She wanted a decent burial without the unnecessary trimmings. Buying a steel vault would fit into this category and was, therefore, out of the question.

Before going to the funeral home Daddy met with us, his children. We agreed to spend no more than $2,000.00 on the total funeral. Imagine our dilemma when we learned that the basic casket cost that much. We looked around until we found a casket that was just a little bit cheaper. The mortician finally convinced us, against our better judgement, to purchase a burial shroud to hide the visual pressure points that would be caused by gravity and the colostomy. (I still wonder about that.)

For the funeral director, the next phase of preparing for the funeral was the decision related to the family flowers that adorn the casket. We were satisfied that we'd given Momma plenty of flowers, and we were not willing to buy one that she couldn't smell. "Just leave it bare," was our request. We offered to bring a plant from the house, but were told that to do so would be tacky. We even argued against using the limousine service; our cousin had a van, and we were sure he'd allow us to use it. The director told us that we probably would be in no shape to drive ourselves to the wake and funeral. We lost this battle and rode in the limousine.

The initial shock of losing a family member to death gives a person certain rights, not legal rights, but the relative authority to display irrational behavior. Basic instinct goes into full swing making ordinary discussions, distractions, and imperatives appear to be mountains. The following is a case in point.

Momma was a member of the Order of Eastern Star (O.E.S.). Except for Momma's instructions that she wear a white dress decorated with her "Star Regalia" and that the regalia should not be buried, we knew nothing else. However, the Worthy Matron went overboard, by our standards, to let us know what had to be done. We weren't exactly appreciative. In fact we were very angry. Daddy told us that we had to allow the O.E.S. rituals to be done appropriately. We listened to him (another offshoot of initial shock) and the O.E.S. carried out their part without a flaw or a missed word. Normally the O.E.S.

protocol wouldn't have bothered me, but I think this event was the proverbial last straw.

The initial shock experience allows the bereaved to receive visitors, make formal arrangements, and form a bond with family both far and near. This transitional phase has no definite life span, but will not end before the final memorial service begins. It is in this time that, except for asking God "Why?" we question everything without questioning anything. We live in the hope that one day we will have hope. It's a very confusing time, not a time for entertaining possibilities that appear to be related to serious decision-making. The shock of death reminds us to make a will, update a will, make our desires known to family and friends, and remember that death will not forget about us.

At the outset, initial shock is a blessing for protection and a nightmare for behavior. Hidden deep within the pain and sorrow is the faithfulness of God that reminds us that God's mercies are new every day. And because of God's faithfulness to us, we can trust God to be whom we need, whenever we need, especially during the moments of initial shock. I had read and heard about God's faithfulness, but it was not until Momma died that I really had to trust in God's faithfulness as an adult.

I marvel at God! When I reflect upon my initial shock, I clearly see God at work. It was during this period that I realized that God really is awesome. Because Momma was only sixty-two years old, the promise of "threescore and ten" (KJV) years of life from Psalm 90 became a real issue for me. Several years passed before I understood that the psalmist was making a declaration that no matter how long or short our time on earth is, we will leave this earth and fly away. We will die. It was then that I realized the truth in Momma's statement about "a hundred years from now, it won't make a difference." Momma knew that her task was to live for God while she could and do all that she reasonably could do for others.

During the first few days, moments, weeks, and months after Momma died, the finality of life became clear to me. I had to learn how to live again, but I didn't know how. There was too much pain. I believed that God had cheated me by taking Momma. I hadn't planned to live life with Daddy and without Momma. How was my relationship with Daddy going to survive our not having Momma around to calm the arguments?

I had to realize that we couldn't be successful in hiding from death. Death will find us. When we are born we immediately begin the process of dying. There is no way around it. This means that all of us will die a physical death. Regardless of how physically fit we are, one day our heart will stop beating; our lungs will not expand and contract, and no blood will flow through our body to provide nutrients. Christians' joy comes in knowing that physical death does not have to mean spiritual death. When Christians die on earth, we go to a life with Jesus that lasts forever.

Death, the cessation of physical life as we know it, makes life worth living. As Christians we are to rejoice in death, not blame people for dying because of unbelief in physical healing or because of unconfessed sin. We die because that is the way all earthly life ends.

When we accept Jesus Christ as our Savior and Lord, our desire is to live so that we will spend eternity in Heaven with Jesus. Because we are human beings who are made of flesh and blood, in order to meet Jesus, we must be changed into another form. The Apostle Paul described the change as our mortal putting on immortality.

All persons can have the joy of a good life after this life. If you have never asked Jesus into your life, do so right now. In your own way talk to God by:

+ Confessing that you are sinner;
+ Telling God that you believe Jesus was crucified and buried and resurrected from the grave to save you from your sins; and
+ Asking Jesus to come into your life and help you to live a righteous life.

Will accepting Christ take away initial shock and other pains in life? No, I can't honestly say that it will. I will promise you that when life hurts, you will find some peace and comfort in knowing that you have a positive relationship with Jesus. This will help you over the little and big hurdles of life, regardless of what they are.

While initial shock provides avenues for public and familial displays of "foot-in-mouth" disease, Christians are called to a higher place in God. Even in grief, when pain speaks, we must temper the sting of our words by being careful not to speak words that hurt others. This was one of Momma's strongest characteristics. She chose her words carefully, not wanting to say anything that couldn't be retracted. It was only after she died that I understood why, but Momma always knew that anything we said could not be completely retracted. We can't erase words and behave as if they never were spoken.

The Funeral

Funerals and memorials are necessary, not for the dead, but for the family members and friends who survive. They provide the final opportunity for the living to say goodbye to the dead and seal the truth that a major transition has begun to unfold. The fact that life must be lived without the deceased becomes real. At this point in time, a little bit of the initial shock begins to crumble. (Although I sometimes believe they are different, in this chapter I will use the terms *funerals* and *memorials* interchangeably.)

While sadness is a part of the grief process, this final memorial can be a time of rejoicing. The services for Christians, those who die after accepting Jesus Christ as their Savior, should be a time of fellowship, worship, and remembrance. Before Momma's death I realized the importance of a service of remembrance. When Momma died I felt an intense need to close this chapter of her life in a way that would have made her proud.

I believe that a service should reflect the deceased person's life. Therefore, it is important to include people who can help the family celebrate the good, even with laughter, while being sensitive and respectful of the seriousness of death. Our Momma lived in the same small town her entire life. We had attended funerals in Clinton, and we knew some of the wrenching agony that went with the territory. We wanted Momma's farewell to be different. We didn't want a sad service; we wanted a party—a celebration of a life that had been lived well in spite of all the emotional and physical pains.

Death rocks the framework of our world. Memorial services are official announcements that a major relational shift has occurred. It is to our advantage to acknowledge this change in the presence of family and friends. I won't argue in favor of either private or public services. Whichever works for the closest relative or friend who knew the deceased best (and accepts responsibility for the financial arrangements) is what should be done. Because family members seek a "bloodline only" private service does not cancel the privilege of friends to hold a separate service.

Momma's funeral was a grand event! Careful planning and a commitment to saying goodbye to Momma in a way that she would have appreciated made us pull out all stops. When my youngest sister and I were developing the program, we both knew that an 8-1/2" x 11" sheet of paper folded once would not meet our needs. That would have been ordinary for Clinton, SC, and being ordinary was not enough for an extraordinary lady. We opted for a long tri-fold program with a photo, Momma's favorite teachings, and her favorite poem.

The night before the service a wake was held at the funeral home where the Order of Eastern Star (O.E.S.) presented their memorial service. We spent two hours greeting people. The difference was that the funeral home was not quiet. People laughed and shared and cried and hugged. This was *not* the Clinton norm, but we, the children, decided that we would not sit and silently look at a corpse until it seemed to breathe. One aunt had a problem with our behavior, but we had to do what we had to do. We felt better, and for us that was the only thing that mattered.

Very early on the morning of the funeral, Momma's casket was placed in the church. My brother created a collage of pictures from Momma's life and placed it in the church too. Because she told us, we knew that Momma wanted the casket closed for the last time prior to the start of the service.

The procession of clergy and family was very long. Of course we came in first: Daddy, children, siblings, nieces, in-laws, cousins, and friends. We sat while others experienced the final viewing. In an effort to "put Momma to bed" one last time, we, her immediate family, closed the casket. As the videographer did his job, we did the following:

+ Shari, Matthew, and Harry turned the crank that lowered the body into the casket;
+ Laurethia removed the Order of Eastern Star regalia;
+ Lovancie pulled the satin cover part of the way across Momma's torso;
+ I pulled the cover further;
+ Bill covered Momma's face;
+ Daddy finished lowering the body into the casket;
+ All of us closed the casket.

This was an emotional time, but we also knew that Momma would have wanted us to behave intelligently.

The services lasted for almost two hours and proceeded without a glitch. Everybody Momma met was special in some way; so our biggest problem was deciding who would speak at the service. Harry, my husband, offered the prayer. A group of cousins sang, and another cousin read a poem. The many remembrances included a man who was like a son, and those who knew Momma as a friend, classmate, co-worker, neighbor, student, employee, church member, and Order of Eastern Star sister. Momma's pastor made remarks. I read the family paper, a series of memorable events and ideas.

Program participants did a thorough job of detailing Momma's life. The sermon was given by one of Momma's former first grade students. There was one time, just after we closed the casket and during the singing of the opening hymn, that we cried real tears really hard but quietly. I believe this was when I realized that Momma's life with us had ended. I think I was numb and somewhat dazed.

I don't remember any feelings breaking through, and if they had tried, my Christian spiritual place would have swallowed them whole. I couldn't allow myself to feel pain, defeat, or loss. To do so would have exposed the softer side of a person who was extremely stoic and in control. I didn't want to say "Hallelujah." I wanted Momma. But, in my spiritual world, no good and faithful Christian would permit such a display of feelings for something that God controlled.

The student in me wanted to know what lesson was to be learned from this process. And the answer came. I learned that funerals seal the reality of physical death. When the casket is closed or the urn or photograph is in place, unless unusually special circumstances arise, there is no chance of seeing the deceased person again on earth. This is closure at its best and worst.

Earlier I mentioned that the funeral service was videotaped. While watching the tape we remembered that Matthew (our son) wasn't around for the repast. Because so many family members were present, we didn't notice his absence. The video showed us that Matthew stayed at the grave while the cemetery workers completed their job. Matthew's eyes shifted between the hole in the ground, the casket, and the men who closed the grave. As a child I always went to funerals; Shari and Matthew had not been to a funeral of a close relative. When I asked four-year-old Matthew why he stayed at the grave, he replied, "If Grandma went to live with God in Heaven, why were they putting her in the ground?"

From Matthew's response I learned that children don't grasp the reality of death. Why should they? Adults don't either. As adults we learn to repeat what we've been told over time but don't necessarily believe. Many of us adult Christians grew up in an age when children didn't question adults. From Santa Claus to the Tooth Fairy, we accepted whatever story the adults in our lives gave us. Even the little doubt that squeezed into our world was choked by fears of what would happen if we dared to ask any questions about almost anything. Today's generation of children laughs at the things we thought were so obviously true. They question everything they're told and believe hardly anything they hear, especially from adults. This is not necessarily bad.

After Momma's death I became so much more aware of the "funeral faith" I recognized in others and myself. "The Lord knows best," sounds holy. We've been taught to believe that God really does know what's best for us. I don't doubt that God knows what's best, but believing the words and living the reality dwell at two different places in life. Funerals lead us on a search for the brighter side of life. In our search for joy—anything that temporarily removes the pain of death—we use old cliches that, when dissected, mean nothing to us, but serve a strong role in getting us through the tough moments by balancing our emotions.

When Momma died I used the "God knows best" cliche so much that I forgot to also accept that even when I believed that God knew what was best, I still hurt. Was the "best" for Momma, my family and me, or all the persons who had been touched by her life? Or was it just for God? There are times when I'm still trying to decide.

The funeral service allowed me to acknowledge that if I could have felt, I would have felt pain. When my faith told me that God had taken Momma out of her misery, I didn't have the courage to say (aloud) to God or anyone else, "But what about my misery?"

Momma's funeral services proved to be a blessing and a curse. I was blessed to share with family and friends and learn what they thought and felt about Momma. The curse came in the videotape. For the first few weeks I watched the tape almost every day, not all of it, but snippets. By the end of July, once or twice a week was all I could take. I think we taped the services so that we would remember. I learned that funerals are for closure, and because it keeps the person alive, continuously watching a videotape of a funeral service can be devastating.

I end this chapter with the following advice. When someone dies and you have a part to play in making the arrangements, please take time to plan the services. Don't allow good-intentioned or fake friends to rob you of this important part of the grieving process. Plan the service so that it reflects the life of the beloved deceased. Protocol can, and should, be respected, but allow the memorial service to be just that—a service that speaks to the memory of the person who died. Blindly following the traditional route, rather than honoring the memory of the deceased, will not remove all the pain, nor will it bring the dead back to life. It will serve a purpose that the survivors will discover much later. Experience has taught me that taking the time to plan the final services helps the grieving process.

Questions

Early in my life I remember wondering if I really belonged to the family with which I lived. Although Momma always expressed pride in me, she did so in a critical kind of way. Even with our strange relationship I needed an explanation for the many questions that surfaced after she died. I explained to myself that Momma wanted the best for all of her children, but my gender and position in the birth order didn't help.

Part of my reasoning for the strange relationship was that I was Momma's project. She was determined to show Peter Moon that my birth had not been a mistake. Through the years Momma was torn between Daddy and the other three children; then there was me, in a world of my own. Yet in a mixed-up way, she loved me and wanted me. She invested in my future and banked on my being a perfect product from Aurelia Dillard Moon's womb. My Aunt Lucile, whom we called Ceal, explained my early years to me. She seems to have been the only person who remembered many of the details or really cared for me, and Momma never disputed her recollections or interfered with her adorations.

I was born at home, delivered by a midwife in the bedroom that I would eventually share with my sisters, at 5:25 A.M. on Saturday, July 19,1958. My daddy wasn't present at my birth, a custom in those days. Because of my low birth weight of four pounds six ounces, I was taken to Hayes Hospital. Each day Ceal would come to the hospital, sit by my bed and cry to my mother, "You're gonna let that baby die." Momma would answer with the promise, "The baby is gonna be just fine." When the worst part of my struggle was over, I was sent home. Most parents probably would have been elated to have their new baby girl doing so much better. However, unless they had to do so, my parents would not hold me. Ceal filled in for them. She held me and cuddled me and loved me back to life.

When I was a toddler, while she attended Saturday classes at Benedict College, my mother would leave me with Granny and Ceal. One day, when I was just a little more than a year old, I began to talk, but I wouldn't talk to Momma or Daddy. I only talked to Granny and Ceal. When Momma was told of how much I had talked while she was away, she was in total disbelief. After all, no child would talk to other people and not to the parents, especially the mother. My aunt and grandma were right, and I continuously refused to talk to anyone else. This game continued for almost two years.

My sister Lovancie was born three months before my third birthday. I saw her for the first time at the hospital where she was born—a family first. Although I remember no preparations being made for this baby's arrival, the image of seeing Lovancie as a newborn remains etched in my mind. She was a pretty baby, and I said that she looked like she had on lipstick.

After Lovancie joined the family at home, I remember a normal family life until one day as I sat on Momma's lap; she told me that I couldn't sit there anymore. The explanation was that her lap was for the new baby. Just as Billy Boy had to move when I was born, my turn had ended. I remember thinking that because one of Momma's legs was shorter than the other, sitting on her lap would cause too much pain. So I watched Lovancie take her rightful place, but Granny and Ceal were still available to enjoy me.

The August after my fourth birthday I started school at Midway Elementary. My name wasn't on the roll; my permanent record had not been created, but I went to school almost every day. Of course I was in Momma's class. School and learning became my comfort zone. I felt more at home with a book in my hand than when the family gathered. Momma was very strict; she made sure that I received no preferential treatment. Actually I was treated worse than the other students. When the culprit of a prank or misdeed couldn't be identified, the blame and punishment clearly belonged and were given to me and me alone.

By not exalting me to the level of "Teacher's Pet" when such an honor seemed obvious to others, Momma was teaching me not to expect breaks in life. She wanted me to know that I would have to work to reach my goals. Her proactive stance was confusing to me; at four years of age I couldn't understand Momma's rationale. One of her co-worker's sons, who was also four, was in school every day too. When his father suggested that we be placed officially in first grade, my momma refused because doing so wouldn't be fair to other children whose parents were not teachers. Without question I spent three long years in first grade with academic records to show for only one. This did nothing to quench my thirst for learning.

One would think that after two years of practice, I would have conquered first grade with all A's. Probably all things being equal except being Aurelia Moon's daughter, I would have soared. Not so in Momma's class. The year that I enrolled in first grade has proven to be the toughest year of my academic life. My grades were nothing to brag about, and I received the low ratings of "4s," the designation for terribly bad, in the non-academic disciplines of behavior, cooperation, self-control, and the like. Momma said she knew I could do the work, so she didn't have to prove it to other teachers. She knew that, if given the opportunity to teach me, they would find out for themselves.

When Momma died I thought a lot about how she treated me when I was one of the students in her classroom each day. That thought led me to realize and accept the fact that according to society's standards I was Momma's black sheep. Perhaps society's standards were right, but to save face and internal turmoil, I interpreted Momma's strange way of relating to me as her way of making me tough.

Very early on she knew that my life was filled with pain from several sources. In our final conversation as mother and daughter, she explained that from my days as a preemie I was a fighter, and she knew I'd make it. Hence, she stood by and watched my personal pain without interfering. Her words, although crafted to be reassuring, reminded me that answers to some questions only evolved into other questions that never would be answered to my satisfaction.

Somehow, I clearly remember wondering why my mother responded to me as she did. Then I willed myself to understand that Momma's intentions should be accepted as honorable. As the oldest girl, I was the one to be dissected. My not being wanted must have driven Momma to extraordinary levels of commitment to make me the best.

In order to bring a product to its best level of performance, extreme measures must be taken. Pruning a tree means cutting its branches, but the eventual beauty shows that the cutting was well worth the effort. An infection in the finger might mean cutting the skin, but the healed finger shows that the cutting was a blessing. The book of Job mentions the main character's being tried in the fire, but the end product of pure gold made the pain of the torrid heat worthwhile.

I mentioned having questions for Momma, but I also had questions for God. I wasn't sure that questioning God was right or safe, but I convinced myself that if I died as a result of my questions, if God gave me only one answer, the end would more than justify the means. As I watched the videotape of Momma's funeral while the reality of her not being with us tried to sink in, I couldn't believe that God actually had taken Momma and left me here with Daddy.

Didn't God realize that Daddy was not the fathering type? Didn't God remember how we saw Daddy treat Momma? Couldn't God see that Daddy was the one who should have died so that Momma and her children could know family joy and peace without the threat of Peter Moon? God *had* to realize that Momma was certainly much easier to get along with than Daddy was. After all, Daddy didn't seem to care about any of us.

As often had been the case, God didn't seem to want to answer my basic question or the follow-ups, at least not to my timing or satisfaction. What was I, the logical information hound, supposed to do? God said, "Wait," not in a voice that I could hear, but a voice that spoke through time. In my confusion and shock, I didn't see that God already had begun to answer me.

One answer came on the day after Momma's funeral. Harry and I were alone in Daddy's house. The telephone rang. When I answered, a female's voice on the other end said, "May I speak to Peter Moon?"

Since my brother received calls at the house too, I asked the question we always asked, "Senior or Junior?"

She responded, "Senior."

I told her that he wasn't there and asked who was calling.

The answer, "His daughter."

"His *what?*" I asked.

"His daughter," she replied.

This is not a direct quote, but it's not far from what I said. "Well I don't know who you are, but I just buried my mother yesterday, and I am Peter Moon's oldest daughter. So you *must not* be important because Momma never told me about you. I *resent* the fact that you would call here with this foolishness. Who are you, and where do you live? I need to know...!"

Since she told me where she lived, I felt obligated to spend time with her. I told Harry that I would be right back, and I got into the rental car and drove to Granddaddy's house on Gary Street in Clinton, South Carolina.

Granddaddy was old and sick and in bed. I burst through the front door and went directly to Granddaddy's room. "Granddaddy, look, a woman just called the house saying that she is Daddy's daughter and that she lives in one of your houses. Which house is it? And why am I just hearing about this now? I promised her that I would pay her a visit today, so tell me which house!"

Jack Moon, not to be shaken by any crisis, stayed in the same position, did not bat an eye, and slowly said, "Baby, everybody knows about that child. Your Momma knew about her and everybody else do too."

"Which house, Granddaddy?!" I interrupted.

"The first house, Baby," he calmly said.

"Thank you. That's all I need to know!" I turned, left the room, entered the hallway, and opened the door. There, standing in front of me, was my angel. I didn't recognize my angel because she looked just like my Aunt Vinnie. After seeing the concern on my face and learning what was going on, she told me that what I was about to do wasn't worth the trouble it would cause. "Think about your children! They need you! Don't do it, Sherita!"

That day Aunt Vinnie saved my life. My head was spinning. I was angry, mad, hurt, disgusted, and filled with every other emotion possible. My mental state was not conducive to healthy behavior. How could Momma have known about this child and not told me? I didn't understand. This was not fair to me.

Months later I realized that God was answering my question. When Momma was sick, we prayed for healing, and God healed. Not only did God heal the physical assault on Momma's body, but God also healed the emotional stress of the embarrassment she must have endured at the hands and from the loins of her husband.

Infidelity is a major marital inhibitor. Knowing about Daddy's (supposedly) other children and knowing or suspecting that others knew must have caused a great strain on Momma's mind and, eventually, her body. Have you ever faced a situation that made eating and digesting food an almost impossible task? Momma died of colon cancer. Although she showed little or no signs of stress on the outside, I am convinced that she carried the stress internally and made herself sick.

If Momma had not died first, she probably would have faced more pain from Daddy's lifestyle. Perhaps she would have lost all of the material possessions for which she had worked so hard. God had a better plan and removed Momma from all the discomfort. As I reflected on this bit of information I realized that, once again, God knew best. But still there was another question. Why was Momma so respectful of and responsive to Daddy?

For most of the time I'd known my parents, their relationship appeared interestingly rocky. Daddy was Jack and Lula Moon's baby son to the fullest extent. He was crude, rude, selfish, disrespectful, and, sometimes, mean to all of us. However, at other times, he was kind, gentle, respectful, and loving. He worked hard for his money and made sure we understood that it was *his* money and he could share it with whomever he chose. Aside from the house note, groceries when he wanted to buy them, and back-to-school clothes, we were not the chosen. Daddy's behavior taught me to hate him in the strongest sense of the word; yet, as a Dillard-Moon (a half-Moon as one of my mother's brothers referred to us) I had to play my role perfectly. And I did.

On the other hand, from where I sat, Momma was caring, gentle, giving, and proud. Childhood polio left Momma with one leg being shorter than the other. She never pitied herself, but I think her drive to be the best and not mess up was rooted and grounded in her being physically challenged. Momma was usually present for us. Even when she was extremely angry with me, she would still be present. Momma neither welcomed nor appreciated my negative comments about Daddy. She did not like bad news. She wanted me to think positively and to know that one day I would be on my own with every opportunity to make my life better.

From my point of view, Momma and Daddy never should have gotten married to each other. What about my being born? I would have happily remained in the remote creases of their individual selves, never seeing the light of day. I could not understand how Momma tolerated Daddy as he did exactly everything that he wanted to do. Momma only complained on the too-rare occasions when she felt she had to do so.

No matter what Peter Moon did, Momma reminded me that he was my daddy and that I should respect him. My mental and sometimes verbal response was that just because *she* had to respect him didn't mean *I* had to do the same. Momma always corrected me while telling me that I wasn't old enough to understand marriage. She had made a commitment, and she was not backing away from her word. She had made an investment that she was certain would pay off. She believed she would win. The only thing I was certain of was that her brain was deteriorating because she had been with my daddy too long.

I think Daddy had a love-hate relationship with Momma. Somewhere within him he was proud to be married to a woman who was college-educated, as his sisters were. But deep in his soul he fought a battle against the demon of his resentment for not having a college degree. He was great at his work, and he, too, had the opportunity to attend college, but I think he felt as if he were somehow second-class to his wife. Daddy's failure to embrace Momma's extroverted behavior was an obstacle that he could have overcome. I am uncertain of whether he succeeded. However, he respected Momma's co-workers when with them or when they called.

Through it all Momma respected Daddy. She did all that she possibly could to turn our emotional hellhole into a home. Except for me, and to some degree with me also, she succeeded. The bottom line is that Momma loved Daddy, and she felt better off with him in her life than without him.

When Momma died, this question of accepting Daddy's misbehavior was magnified and was even more difficult for me to ignore. God, knowing the degree of difficulty I experienced, answered the question a few years later when Harry and I went through a rocky time in our marriage. I weighed all the options and prayed and fasted and prayed some more. At times I wanted to leave, but, except for once, my heart said, "No, I'm staying here!"

It was then, a couple of years after Momma died, that I began to understand this game called marriage. I realized that life is always filled with good and bad experiences and that the joy of the journey is in experiencing life to the fullest degree possible. I cannot be shaken from my belief that Jesus came so that I could have the abundant life. Because of my belief, I don't condone mental or physical abuse of any kind. Yet nobody has the right, as I thought I did with my mother, to tell any adult how to operate his or her life. Living is personal. When Momma died I understood this slowly but clearly.

Questions are a part of living. Many people have faced the pain of the "wrong" person's death, family secrets, and relational imbalances. There are times, and I think death qualifies as such a time, when questioning God is acceptable. Our finite minds cannot comprehend most of what God does. Even when we try to refrain from asking, the questions still come. Momma often told me that no human being is responsible for his physical appearance or circumstances of birth. God used Momma's death to remind me of the latter.

We must understand that when we ask questions, God has a choice in answering us. When we ask and sincerely seek answers to our questions, we should stop looking for lightning bolts, tumultuous storms, and blows to the body. God, like angels, often answers in the rainbows of reassurance in small things. Often the answers are disguised as problems and obstacles.

I have many more questions, some of which I am afraid to think, let alone ask. No matter what my questions might be now or later, if I continue to trust God, the answer will come or remain hidden as God sees the need. For this I thank God.

In this age of dysfunctional families—I believe all families fit this description—I now realize that Momma did the best she knew how. Only when Momma died did I really begin to parent. As I took up the mantle of motherhood I began to see that parenting, unlike most other tasks, has no recipe that guarantees that our children will turn out a certain way when certain ingredients are combined and blended properly. Parenting teaches that all children of the same two biological parents are different, sometimes extremely so.

This calls for knowledge of and an attempt to understand each child as a distinct individual. The good news is that God created us to be in relationship with one another. Parenting requires trusting God and believing that God sends friends and enemies our way to show us how to be the best we can be in all areas of life. What we as parents think is best often leads our children to question our love, trust, and respect for them. As parents we must always remind our children that we love them and are willing to give our best for them. Children must see that even when we are not sure what is best, we are willing to seek counsel through prayer to our heavenly parent. I believe that when we trust God to know what is best for all of us and provide all that we need, God will take us where God wants us to be.

Angry and Alone

When Momma died I thought that life would swing back into balance very soon. Other people grieved. I was different. I would be the shining example of how I would not be overtaken by grief. Just as I handled the doctor's news of Momma's pending death very well, the actual death would be just another piece of information to process. At the funeral I was the one person who had the courage and strength to read the family paper without shedding a tear. The aftermath of her death would be just another opportunity for me to witness for Jesus.

When Momma died I immediately began to process paperwork: hospital bills, insurance claims, creditors, annuity transfers to Daddy, and mailing death certificates. I was amazed at the amount of paperwork I was able to complete before returning to Maryland. At least one of my siblings questioned my actions.

"Why are you doing this for him?"

"Because it is the right thing to do."

"He wouldn't do it for you."

"That's beside the point. Remember, it's not how other people treat you that counts; it's how you treat other people. Plus, I don't want Momma visiting me and messing with my sleep," I said with a chuckle.

It seemed very clear that my role as the oddball in charge of trying to keep this fragile and shaky family together was being established. Momma had been the family glue, and somebody had to fill that role. No agreement was written on paper or carved in stone, but I automatically fell into that role.

A little more than one month after Momma died, Laurethia graduated from college. I promised her that I would attend the ceremony even on short notice. To allow Shari to get credit for attending school that day, I picked up my aunt Phine from her house and we left Friday afternoon in order to attend this big event on Saturday, the day before Mother's Day. I dreaded the trip, but I never considered *not* going. I just knew that Momma would have lived long enough for this great celebration had it been within her power, but she died. As a family we would weather this new phase of torment.

The eight-hour drive was emotionally taxing, but with Phine in the car, I always had someone who was awake. We talked about many things, people, and events. Momma was not a topic. Having faced this same pain twenty-two years earlier, Phine must have known my pain. This trip was her first visit with her only remaining sister. I'm not sure that Shari or Matthew thought about what was going on with me, but they probably noticed that I was extremely tense.

After leaving Phine at Ceal's, the children and I went to Daddy's house. Although I returned to the house one week after Momma's death when Harry and I drove to South Carolina to get our children, this time was different. Momma's absence seemed so undoubtedly present.

The house was so different. No furniture had been moved. The décor was the same, but the house had lost much of its flavor. Since we arrived late that night, I wasted no time in getting my children ready for bed. The most painful part of the evening was not being able to say "Good night" to Momma. After I prayed and crawled into bed I marveled that Momma's smell was still there. Since Daddy had the house thoroughly cleaned, her smell must have been in my mind; yet it was so very real.

The next morning, Saturday, started with an early breakfast for everyone and then the drive to Columbia. I don't remember how the carpool was arranged, but we did arrive in Columbia. We were joined by Daddy, Bill, Ceal, Phine, Laurethia's friend Vernard, Aunt Bannah, Aunt Vinnie, our cousin Barbara (Aunt Bannah's daughter) and her children, Sandra, Thomas, and Chris, and Bill's lady friend.

Since we were Laurethia's cheering section, we settled into our seats in the college's Human Resources Center. As a graduate and former employee of Benedict, there was much socializing on my part. I wasn't really focused on the people with whom I talked, but talking was the one way that I could steady myself—keeping busy. Many of my former co-workers expressed their condolences about Momma's death. I graciously accepted their expressions of sympathy and probably talked with more people that day than I did in any month that I'd spent as a Benedict student or staff member.

The line began to form for the processional. Shari, Matthew, and I visited with Laurethia. Without saying so, this was my way of checking my little sister's emotional state. When our time together became too much for me, I returned to my seat. As the graduates began to enter the gym, Laurethia and I made eye contact, but we were careful not to linger.

The ceremony was a usual graduation with few, if any, miscues. We took photos of Laurethia seated and then receiving her diploma. In our myriad of emotions Bill and I greeted her when she left the stage. After the graduates left the building our entire family posed for a picture in front of the Learning Resources Center. There we were, doing what we'd learned to do all of our life—wearing plastered, plastic smiles that covered the pain of what was supposed to be a joyous moment. After dinner at a local restaurant and more photos, we returned to Clinton. The day had proven to be terribly long and well worth the stress. The next day would be Mother's

Day, our first without Momma. Of course I had a plan to help me keep my sanity.

As promised to my passengers and myself, exactly at 6:00 A.M. on that horrible morning in May, I pulled out of the driveway on South Bell Circle. I drove around the curve to Ceal's house. We visited Momma's grave, and by 6:15 A.M., Phine, Shari, Matthew, and I were on our way back to Maryland.

My mind was working overtime. Harry had told me that he was preparing dinner as a part of a Mother's Day treat. I made it clear that I wanted no celebration, and we agreed on dinner. Harry reminded me that my pain did not take away our children's desire to celebrate Mother's Day with me. He was very right.

The drive from Clinton, South Carolina, to Clinton, Maryland, was happening too quickly. By the time we stopped to eat in Burlington, North Carolina, we were making record time. I realized that my adrenaline was pumping at a high rate and I needed to regulate it immediately. After the meal I drove at a much slower speed, but my thoughts accelerated. I didn't feel angry and alone, I *thought* angry and alone.

My children were with me, and they were expressive with their Mother's Day greetings. Remembering Harry's advice, I gladly received the well-wishes from Shari and Matthew, but my mind was stuck in the reality that I could not see or talk with Momma. This knowledge and first experience without her were grueling. The visit to her grave that morning sustained me in the fantasy of having been with her that day. I just wanted to get home where I could be with Harry.

We arrived on Keystone Avenue just before 3:00 P.M.. True to his word, Harry had cooked a delicious meal of chicken, yams, string beans, rice, and dessert. The dining room table was elegantly set with our formal wedding china, stemware, and flatware. To my disappointment we had company—something I neither expected nor wanted. The presence of guests increased my stress level tremendously, but after crying and setting my mind to enjoy the evening, I succeeded in faking again.

That day, Mother's Day 1991, was a horribly beautiful day. The horror was in missing Momma. The beauty was in Shari and Matthew's joy and appreciation for celebrating Mother's Day with me. I responded honestly to their questions about my tears. As their daddy had taught them, they responded with strong hugs and extremely wet kisses.

I was grateful for Harry's concern, yet I knew there was no way possible for him to totally understand. He had gone to great lengths to prepare a scrumptious meal that would help take away my involuntary pain for that day. Overall I enjoyed the food and flavor of the afternoon. Spending time with my husband and children reminded me that I still had people who took time to show me that they cared about me. Once again Harry's generously loving acts helped me survive.

The day's pain was everywhere. I wanted to talk with Momma, and I wanted Momma to talk with me. I didn't want to talk to who was or who used to be. With all my heart, I wanted to reach out and touch Momma. I wanted to hear her voice.

Later that evening I went against every grain of common sense in my body. I remembered that when I preached my initial sermon in October 1989, Momma made remarks at the end of the worship service. While Harry was away at church I found the videotape of that event, put it in the VCR and saw and heard Momma talk about me. Afterward my thoughts were angrier and more alone. In getting my wish of seeing Momma alive on Mother's Day, I betrayed myself.

Momma always enjoyed Mother's Day. Yes, she enjoyed life, but Mother's Day was special. When Granny died I knew that Mother's Day was never the same for Momma. Subsequent years brought a different type and degree of difficulty, but I didn't know how difficult those times were until Momma died. Almost ten years have passed, and I still have not found a word that adequately expresses my feelings.

Not that another time would have been better, but Momma's cancer was not diagnosed at a good time for my personal family in Maryland. As pastor of Union Bethel African Methodist

Episcopal Church in Brandywine, Maryland, my husband Harry was under the stress of overseeing the building of a new sanctuary. Therefore, in my own way, so was I. Actual construction began in July 1990. As the project's completion neared, the Moons' plan was to attend Laurethia's graduation. Then Laurethia and Momma would come to Maryland, and my children and I would join them on a trip to New York City, a place where Momma had not been before. All of us would return to Maryland and celebrate the dedication of the new church edifice.

Of course Momma's death forced a major change in our plans. The post-graduation trip was cancelled, but the dedication service went on as scheduled. To ease my thought process for that day, I appealed to family and friends to contribute to an offering that would be presented to Union Bethel in memory of Momma. On Dedication Day, the second Sunday in July 1991, Ceal, Phine, Laurethia, Vernard, along with other friends and my family stood as Bill presented the funds to Union Bethel. He mentioned how badly Momma wanted to see the new Union Bethel, but God had other plans. Because Momma wasn't there and because I wanted her to be there so badly, my thoughts focused on how alone I was. Being surrounded by biological, legal, and faith families did not erase my angry emptiness at being so alone.

On July 19, 1991, I celebrated my thirty-third birthday. When I was a child at home, Momma would wake me up at 5:25 A.M., the time that I was born, and sing "Happy Birthday." On the first birthday that I celebrated as a married lady, the ritual continued. Harry was stunned and thought this tradition to be strange. However, for this special occasion he learned to temper the early morning assault by putting the telephone on my side of the bed.

For as long as I remembered, Momma called and sang to me. But in 1990, the last year that Momma was alive on my birthday, she did not call me. She said she overslept. One year later I couldn't help but wonder whether Momma knew she wouldn't be here to celebrate and in her own way wanted to help me make the adjustment. Whatever the reasoning, I felt angry and alone on what usually was my special day. My husband, children, and I celebrated with the night ending in the final dedication worship service for the new Union Bethel sanctuary. Nothing erased the hurt of Momma's not being present to celebrate with me.

Being angry and alone took its toll on me. As an adult, I was so unaccustomed to having to accept such pain. I was lost. My world was out of control because Momma was not here to help me. Other areas of life were filled with joy and happy moments, but I wanted Momma. I was too angry and too alone! My efforts to improve my status ended in failure. I would make more mistakes that would set me back a few paces from being comforted.

In my mature state I know now that God was with me, keeping me alive and sane. My strong desire to touch and see Momma did not diminish. I refused to accept the truth that Momma was not coming back. Being alone was safe; being angry was dangerous. I had to mediate my situation and reach a better conclusion than I thought I faced. I needed God's help more than ever, but most of the time, I forgot to ask for it. At other times, I was too angry with God to seek God's help. I blamed God for my pain. Wasn't God responsible for Momma's death and my being angry and alone?

The words from Acts 17:28, "for in Him we live and move and have our being," were familiar to me, but unimaginably painful to read or hear. God made us and knows us. All humans were made with a desire to seek God. God is never far from us; we do live and move and are because of God. In my loneliness I needed God, but my anger blinded me from seeing God. I wanted somebody that God had chosen to take away from me. I was a hopeless case. I didn't want to be angry or alone, but, to me, my options were limited to these two positions. I had no idea that matters in my life would get much worse before they showed any sign of improvement.

Big Mistakes

With the new church built and occupied, Harry embarked on a vacation that would last the entire month of August. After the first Sunday's worship services, Harry, Shari, and Matthew left for South Carolina. Upon entering our house and praying for their safe journey, I busied myself with housework. Then I started my vacation.

As was customary, I picked up the telephone, dialed the number and waited for Momma to answer so that I could tell her that my family was on the way to South Carolina. On the fourth ring, I began to unravel. I realized that Momma would not answer the phone this time, or ever again. I slammed the receiver back onto the cradle only to have it fall, but I didn't care. My head began to ache; my hands were shaking, and my entire body joined the process. I felt dizzy, almost faint, and sweat poured from my body. My knees were weak. Finally I sat on the carpet in front of the sofa and cried. Except for the night of Momma's funeral, and then to a much lesser degree, I had never cried out in grief. When the tears ended, my face was swollen and clammy. Red blotches decorated my arms and legs. I was exhausted beyond belief. I got up, hung up the phone, and gently allowed my body to sink into the pillows on the sofa where I slept until the early hours of the following morning.

The cerebral me had to have an explanation. During my brief period of self-analysis, I understood that in my continuous and devoted efforts not to grieve as those who have no hope, I had not grieved at all. The aftermath of Momma's funeral was followed by my immediate return to work, Annual Conference, the end of the school year for Shari and me, the church construction and dedication, and my birthday. In my assurance that I had always handled death well, grieving was never placed on my personal agenda.

Until Momma died, I never knew how central she was to our family. Within four months the family relationship had changed dramatically, almost to the point of being totally destroyed. I, and I believe the same was true for my siblings, did not feel as if I belonged to *any* family. And the worst was yet to come.

On the weekend of August 9, 1991, I was with my family in Swansea, South Carolina, visiting my in-laws. I rented a car and drove to Clinton with my children in tow. Renting the car was Harry's idea, just in case things didn't go right. As I left the rental agency, Harry gave me a bail card, from our motor club, and laughed that he hoped I wouldn't need it.

When I arrived in Clinton late Friday night I went to the old homestead. I am not sure whether I told Daddy I would be there. Even though his car was not visible I wasn't worried; I still had my key to the front door. To my surprise, the front screen door was locked. I went to the back door. The storm door was unlocked, but my key wouldn't fit in the back door. This was my first time in Clinton since Laurethia's graduation, and to say that I was ticked off is an understatement.

The children and I stayed at Ceal's house that night. The following morning I called Daddy to tell him we were in town; we exchanged pleasantries. He invited us to come to his house where we had a great day together. I suggested to Laurethia, who was living in Mauldin, and Bill that we meet with Daddy that night. After telling me that this was a bad idea, they consented to go along with my suggestion.

We gathered at Daddy's house that evening. I started the meeting by saying how hurt I was to find the house door locked. I explained that Momma always made us feel welcome and that their house was our house. Although their realistic thoughts were ahead of my lofty dreams of conciliation, my siblings were in total agreement. We expressed our concern at not having a place to call home anymore.

Somewhere in our list of demands that were disguised as requests, Daddy kindly interrupted and asked what would satisfy us. Almost simultaneously we said in one form or another "having a key and access to this house." Daddy responded, "When your momma died, the first thing I did after they [the morticians] took her body from the house was have Sherita read the will. The will made it clear that everything your momma left was mine, including the house and her car. Now before you (pointing at me) and your chaps left after the funeral, I offered you the chance to get whatever you wanted from your momma's stuff. You took what you wanted. Then I come home a few weeks ago and all my stuff is missing. I'm here wondering who took all my stuff. I knew who had it so I said, all right they got it. Now, this here is *my* house! Y'all are welcome to come here anytime you get ready when I'm here, but you are *not* getting a key to come in here when I ain't home and steal my stuff! Now that's right!"

I was so angry that I literally jumped from my chair and said, "I don't believe you've said this! You're telling us that we don't have a place to call home anymore! It's just not the same! It's not fair!" I blabbed on and on, not listening, or more accurately, not heeding my siblings' advice to forget this and move on. When Daddy got tired of listening to me he went back to his room, and I followed immediately with my siblings and offspring close behind.

Each step was punctuated by an increase in my temper. I spouted off about how Daddy *always* hated us, *never* was there for us, *used* us, *abused* us, and now that he had gotten rid of Momma, he finally was doing what he always wanted to do: hanging us out to dry. I let everybody present know that I would not accept this vain bully's decision peacefully.

As Daddy left his room he suggested that I was crazy. At that remark, my blood began to boil to the point where I seemed to actually feel my blood moving inside of me. Daddy headed toward the kitchen, and I got close to his face and began to back him into a corner. In search of freedom he opened the back door and stepped out into the laundry room area. I yelled and fussed about anything that came near my mind. I didn't care who heard me. Nothing mattered except my desire to get back at him for what (I believed) he had done to Momma and what (I believed) he was doing to us. I remember throwing raw eggs and canned cat food from the back door into the yard. The fact that my son imitated me had no bearing on my behavior.

My ability to reason was gone, and I was not interested in bringing it back. Nothing and everything mattered. I missed Momma, and Daddy was not my idea of a parent. Because he had not been around us as much as Momma had been, he could not understand us, and I was not going to allow him to take away the memories of Momma's good or bad influence in my life.

That night's confrontation was not a good thing. I went to bed holding much hatred toward Daddy and God. My disposition toward the former was based on what I saw and heard. My attitude toward the latter actually sprang from what I felt, but I traced it to what I thought. My life was hanging in midair, and since closure is important to me, I needed the assurance of knowing that the previous night's activities were a part of history. To this end, before leaving for church the following morning, I requested another family meeting. Daddy consented, and, although they didn't like my idea, Bill and Laurethia agreed to go back to Daddy's house with me that night.

In church I mentioned to Bill that my hand was hurting and a bit swollen. Bill said, "When we get home [meaning Daddy's house] I'll show you why." True to his word, I followed Bill to Daddy's room where Bill pointed to the bedroom door, and said, "This is why your hand hurts. Last night you punched this hole in this door." I was surprised, but, in a sick way, I was proud.

After church my children, Ceal, and I joined Daddy for dinner at a local restaurant. We went back to Daddy's house, changed clothes, and visited a few relatives and friends. Bill and Laurethia arrived at the agreed-upon time. We gathered in the den again, probably in the same self-assigned seats. Sitting in different chairs would have meant that something must have been wrong the night before. Being Moons, we couldn't and, therefore, wouldn't admit to any wrongdoing on our part.

The conversation was similar to the previous night. We three Moon children wanted carte blanche access to the house of our childhood, and Peter Moon wasn't budging. As we talked, I was proud that the conversation was so much better than the night before. In my state of passive gratitude, I didn't remember to seek God's guidance. Since we weren't making much progress, and being a person who didn't believe in wasting time, I barked, "Daddy, since you won't do what *we* ask, what do *you* want? What would make *you* happy with *us*?"

He answered, "What do I want? I want you to get your stuff and get …out of my house!"

I said, "You just cussed in the presence of my children. I know you don't care about *us*, but don't you care what your *grandchildren* think about you?"

He was quick with, "I don't care what anybody thinks!"

"Not even your grandchildren?" I asked.

Daddy fired back with, "I want y'all out of my house."

Confusion took control. I could not believe that we were behaving like this again. While Daddy and I yelled back and forth to each other, my siblings and I took items from the house that held a special meaning for us. Then Daddy went back to his bedroom. I don't remember seeing my children; my eyes were fixed on Peter Moon, Sr. Knowing that he kept his gun in his bedroom, I followed him. If any bullets were fired, I would be the martyred target. Instead Daddy went to his safe, and when I saw him take out papers, I was relieved enough to walk away.

The next time I saw Daddy, he was sitting in a rocking chair in front of the fireplace in the living room. He smiled and said, "I just called the police on y'all."

"Sure you did!" I snapped.

In less than ten minutes, his warning became a reality. Members of the Clinton Police Department were in the living room, and I wasn't about to back down from these people who usually carried badges, guns, and clubs. Laurethia told me later that my refusal to stop yelling led one cop to promise me a "place to spend the night" if I said one more word. The police stayed until we left. We spent the night at Laurethia's apartment.

The following morning brought a new kind of hope for me. Laurethia said she was committed to honoring Daddy's command to stay away from his house. My anger eased, and, after visiting my three aunts in Clinton, I went back to Swansea.

Now, even more than ever, home for me would be Clinton, *Maryland*. Why? It was the place where mortgage payments allowed me a key and total access. And since I had no parent to invite me to the home of my birth, a place where memories thrived, I was relieved.

When Momma died, I experienced many thought processes. Having never been so close to death's pain made for a mental fiasco. Throughout Momma's various illnesses and physically weak moments, thinking and reading always provided escapes. To my unending horror, Momma's death couldn't be thought away or read away. No mental exercise provided the answer to unthinkable or unspeakable questions. The books that I read were perfect for people who needed to grieve. Since I didn't think I belonged in that category, I found no solace for my aching mind. Armed with no answers from God, I fought my battle with all that I knew. I, Sherita Gayle Moon Seawright, would will myself to be where I thought I needed to be. A period of reflecting was not to come until several years later, but honesty would be a necessary element.

I decided that my siblings and family needed me to hold the family together just as Momma had done. Wasn't I smart enough, tough enough, and brave enough to take up where Momma left off? As the oldest girl, wasn't this my predestined role? My decision to take on a monumentally impossible task formed the master plan for my martyrdom.

Cerebral living is great in the classroom. Textbook, pens, and paper allow for unlimited creativity in "the shoulds," what should have been. Life, at its best, cannot be lived exclusively in the brain's intellectual realm. My first six months of life after Momma's death proved this fact with no holds barred. I learned a lot, but even then, especially then, being able to let go of the thinking realm was very difficult. I planned to win this war with my mind. Since nobody's mind was sharper, this journey would be an open-and-shut case.

As I examine my experiences of 1991, everything seems much clearer now. The fog that blocked my view has lifted. The first lesson I saw was that I was wrong in many ways. The following examples describe only a few of my mistakes.

I misinterpreted the Holy Scriptures. The Apostle Paul's writings to the Thessalonians meant that we who know Christ and have a relationship with Him do not grieve as those who do not know Christ, and therefore have no hope of eternal life with Jesus. I interpreted Paul's messages as a command for the saved to rejoice and not grieve at all. Paul's instruction clearly does not remove the grieving process. He gives Christians permission to grieve while experiencing the joyous hope and expectation of seeing our beloved again.

While the Christian does grieve, the process is very different from those who are unsaved. Persons who have not accepted Jesus as their Savior will only see a dead body, the shell that once held vibrant life. For the saved, the empty shell represents a burden that has been shed, left behind because it is no longer needed. Christians grieve the physical loss of contact, but we don't get stuck in the grief place forever. At some point, in spite of our grief, we realize that our life must continue. We rejoice in knowing that our relative, who also had a positive relationship with Jesus, is experiencing a new life; therefore, we celebrate in the hope of spending eternity with Jesus and our loved ones.

Secondly, I thought that my pain was mental when, in fact, it was emotional. As a child I learned that emotions were dangerous. Showing any sign of pain only gave my superiors permission to hurt me more. Thirty-two years later I was still at that same spot, knowing that God chose to pick on little old me to prove a point to everyone else. How paranoid and small-minded could I have been?

Everything continued to be a thought, a battle of the mind. When Momma died, I masked what must have been the emotional pain. I didn't know that doing so would prolong and worsen the time spent at my lowest point. Any sign of a feeling could have been and probably was tucked away.

Parents, please allow your children to grieve. In the many tragedies that are described as horrible at best, this generation of children must learn how to grieve. The trials of today's cultures, societies, and realities do not leave room for the stiff upper lip.

Boys need to cry; the process of acknowledging the need for a release makes a better man. Learning to cry as a boy must not be labeled as bad. Boyhood tears don't last forever; many smiles will replace the pain. In adulthood the memories of the crying and smiling cycle give hope that regardless of my situation, God will allow me to smile again, just as before.

Recently I tried to purchase an item that, less than fifteen years ago was very visible and indicative of proper attire: ladies' handkerchiefs. Until I visited an upscale store, I had no success. As I thought about this phase of my writing, there seemed to be a message and correlation. Modern girls have been taught to be tough. The feminine touch is not popular. A tiny handkerchief fades in light of the big hankie that absorbs the tough male's sweat. Girls of all ages need to know that a time comes when a woman's handkerchief is necessary. When Momma died, a handkerchief would have been a tremendous asset to me. However anticipating and permitting tears could not break through my feminist and womanist thoughts. Surviving death is one time when our emotional nature should be allowed to take its course with unlimited freedoms.

The weekend of August 9, 1991 provided many additional learning experiences for me. Several years passed before I wanted to acknowledge the lessons. Yes, they are painful but have not lost any of their power. Eating crow is not one of my favorite activities, but I've eaten much of this "delicacy" since Momma died.

As I reflect on that horrible two-day period in August, I realize that I had no right to demand access to anything that belonged to anybody else. In her giving everything to Daddy, Momma made sure that our ride as spoiled brats was over. Was Momma right to make us think that the family home was also ours? Was Daddy wrong to tell us that what we knew as the family home was no longer ours? A strong "No!" rises within me. Both parents made choices, one that pleased the offspring and one that brought a tremendous degree of displeasure to the same. Both parents were satisfied with their particular choice.

The bottom line is that our demanding a key and unlimited access to Daddy's house was wrong. We never returned the items that we took that hot August night, and, in response to my inquiry, Daddy told me that he did not want them. No, he didn't tell us of his plans for a lockout. He must have recognized advance notice as an undesirable option. On the other hand, had we respected his decision, eventually he might have changed his mind. Now, we have no family homestead. Those of us who still talk to our male parent visit at *Daddy's* house.

My behavior, though emotionally unhealthy, was not what I would consider becoming to an adult child, a parent, or a Christian. Although I'd like to think otherwise, my Christian witness was horrible. My behavior was a terrible reflection on the Christian way of life that Jesus promoted. It did not bring glory to God at all. Instead Satan's power and influence were brought to a higher level, and only Satan could rejoice. Yes, I needed to express myself, but I know that I could and should have done so in a way that would have been much more representative of the Christian lifestyle.

I learned that Christians must be prepared for trials. Expecting a battle and not being prepared for battle are two very distinct states of mind. David killed Goliath because David knew his enemy, located his enemy, and trusted God to bring victory. In my case, I knew Daddy was being defensive, thereby making him my enemy. Just as in David's case, I knew where the enemy was located. Unlike David and much to my shame, I did not seek or trust God for victory over this enemy. Of all the fallout from Momma's death, this loss was the greatest. It has divided my family of origin. So much bad was said and done that only God can work the miracle of reconciliation. Lord, I believe.

The Stepparent

After the incident in August 1991, I had very few dealings with Peter Moon. At that time in my life, I promised never to be hurt again by the man who donated the sperm for my existence. Because I like to bring closure to all situations, making the promise was easy. Keeping the promise was a struggle.

My Clinton, South Carolina, connection was not lost. My brother was there and I kept in touch with my three aunts. Except for my brother, the others often asked whether I talked with Daddy. Finally they accepted the reality that I would not talk with him. For many months, my heart was torn. Not talking to Daddy seemed to be the grown-up impressionable response that satisfied my youngest sister. As far as I was concerned, not talking to Daddy was wrong, and the little girl inside of me ached for the strength to be vulnerable again. I had only one living parent, and I didn't want to lose him.

When Momma died, I wondered whether Daddy would remain a widower. In error I thought I saw the answer very early. On one of my visits to Clinton after Momma died, I went to a local fast food restaurant. As I was leaving, I noticed a familiar car pulling into a parking space. Daddy and a lady were coming to this restaurant in what I considered to be Momma's car.

Upon looking at the lady I recognized her as a lady who befriended my mother at a class reunion. That was it! My parking lot manner was not good. I yelled at Daddy, telling him how he was disrespecting Momma. I made a scene until God sent a cousin who grabbed me, held me back and told me to "Let it go!" I followed her instructions and went to my maternal aunt's house.

Much of my time was devoted to not communicating with Daddy personally. This was not my most comfortable *modus operandi*. To keep abreast of local news, in general, and property transfers, in particular, I subscribed to my hometown weekly newspaper. One day in 1994 as I was reading the paper, I turned to the community column that Momma used to write. Almost immediately some words caught my eye, "Rev. and Mrs. Peter Moon…" My breathing became shallow, and I said to Harry, "I have a stepmother!" Harry looked at me. I don't remember his response.

Saying the word "stepmother" was an out-of-body experience. Although I knew I was speaking, the sounds must have come from another source. For me, *stepmother* was a bad word; I'd seen so many cases where stepmothers were either hated or ignored or both. In my psyche, stepmothers were bad news. As my mind vacillated from good to evil, another thought slapped me. Why hadn't I heard this before? I learned of my stepmother's existence by reading the newspaper. I began to investigate.

I called Bill first, and, of course I didn't get an answer. I called Laurethia and was greeted by her answering machine. I was certain that contacting these siblings would provide the information that I wanted and, at that time, needed. Finally I was successful in contacting Bill. Our conversation was very simple.

"Bill, I just read that we have a stepmother."

"I know that," he said.

"You know?" I retorted.

He stated, "Yeah."

My next question was, "Why didn't somebody tell me?"

Bill explained, "You had a whole lot of problems with Daddy, and we thought it would be better if you didn't know. We didn't know how you would act; so we didn't tell you." His "we" statements really hurt.

Although I understood their reasoning, and respected their choice, privately, I was hurt! Was I still the outcast? Had my differences with Daddy meant limited communication with my other family members? Why didn't somebody think or remember that I wanted to know family news?

A short while later, Ivy, my stepmother, called our house. She told Harry that she wanted to meet us and become friends with us. Harry told her that for right now we'd appreciate her not contacting us. The silence was sealed.

Laurethia wanted nothing at all to do with Ivy. She only needed to know that Ivy was married to the man who told all of us to get out of his house. With this in her mind, neither Ivy nor Daddy existed.

Learning that I had a stepmother did not have a negative effect on me. My consolation came in knowing that Daddy was legally married. When Momma was alive, he had other women in various places; now at least he was legal again. I did think about his wandering tendencies, but that wasn't my business.

I also wondered about my stepmother. There must have been more to this marriage than met the eye. Women in Clinton, South Carolina knew my daddy too well to actually commit to living with him as his wife.

As my information base expanded, I found out that Daddy's wife was from the island country of Jamaica by way of New York. Aha! She didn't know him. I continued to reflect on Ivy's telephone call to us in Maryland, her wanting to meet us and become friends. Why would she marry a man with four children who have nothing to do with their daddy? Only time would tell, and since I wasn't talking to Daddy, the time would not arrive soon.

In August 1997 while my family and I were in South Carolina, a strange series of events led to my meeting Ivy. She received me with a warm hug and a big smile. I liked her immediately. She seemed genuinely warm, loving, and sincere. I still wondered why she married my daddy.

When Momma died, I never imagined having a stepmother. I was certain that Daddy would live out his days without a signed commitment to anyone. His being a widower would be ideal for him. News of his marriage was a shock, but I wasn't angry that he got married again. My anger was in not having been told the news.

Reflecting on my behavior in response to Daddy's relationship with women soon after Momma died left me feeling ashamed. I learned lessons from this phase of my life. The following provides a sampling.

When a spouse dies, the spouse is dead. My behavior toward Daddy and the woman with whom I saw him at the fast food restaurant was wrong. I had no right to question his actions or make a scene. *So what* if she had befriended my mother? Momma was dead, and Daddy was released to live again. Also I learned that the lady was not in Momma's car. Upon her death, Momma relinquished her need for ground transportation, and her Last Will and Testament gave the car to Daddy.

For some people the married life is the only happy life; the single life is not for them. For at least two years, except for seeing his son and sometimes his youngest daughter (who totally ignored him) my daddy had no positive or negative interaction with his dead wife's children. For whatever reason, he married again. After three years of widowhood, he did what he wanted to do.

Timing is important. A few years ago, and probably to a lesser extent now, the surviving spouse was bound by society's unwritten rule of "waiting long enough" before remarrying or even dating. With Daddy I was caught in the "not long enough" mode. How dare he be with someone else so soon after Momma died? What nonsense! People need to be free to do what needs to be done in their lives. External restrictions from people who do not understand a person's way of dealing with life can be strangling. During long illnesses before physical death takes a spouse or loved one, the healthy partner sees the pending death and begins to grieve before the moment of death actually comes. As a Christian, my role was to celebrate that Daddy had found companionship, not demean him for doing so in what I thought was too little time.

I also learned that bad pride is dangerous. Since I am convinced that a healthy sense of self is important for survival, I agree with the Holy Scriptures and accept the fact that thinking too highly of oneself is deadly. Seeing Daddy with someone else was a blow to my ego. My thoughts were completely negatively selfish. If my cousin had not rescued me at the restaurant, I probably would have been arrested.

On that particular morning, my entire body was in stress mode. I was willing to risk my freedom for such an insignificant event. I didn't want people to think that my mother would condone such disrespectful behavior from my father. I was also afraid that people would say things such as, "No surprise; he did it when she was alive. Why should anyone think he'd wait?"

In retrospect, I know that Momma did tolerate his lack of respect for their marriage vows. With clear evidence of Daddy's infidelity, she accepted and condoned his cheating ways by staying with him. Who was I to try to stop a widower from behaving as a widower? The time had come for me to stop pouting, grow up, and accept the reality that Daddy had the legal and moral rights to date anyone he wanted and to do so according to his plan.

The final point of this learning experience has proven to be the biggest surprise. My stepmother is a wonderful lady. I am not swayed by what my siblings or other relatives might think. My assessment comes from my limited association with her. As far as I am concerned, Ivy is a kind lady who has a lot of love to share.

The similarities with Momma are astounding. Ivy is a retired teacher with adult children. Her birthday is two days before Momma's. She is quiet and strong. I honestly can say that

Ivy has only been respectful and loving toward my husband, my children, and me. I ask for nothing more.

From my vantage point, my stepmother has been good for my daddy. He doesn't like being told what to do, but I can see slight changes for the good in him that can only be attributed to her influence and our prayers. He spends time with his wife. He takes her out for meals, and he enjoys being with his grandchildren and with his children who are willing to be a part of his life. He still is a notorious pack rat, but at least he wears his hearing aid sometimes.

Do I still wonder about my stepmother? Yes, I do. I wonder how she continues to live in peace with Daddy. I wonder if she'll be able to stay in this marriage until death ends the union. In my daddy and stepmother I see a diluted version of Daddy's relationship with Momma, and that makes me uncomfortable. But, the ins and outs of their relationship do not fall in the realm of my personal affairs.

A stepparent can be a blessing. I happily and honestly say that my stepmother is. Christians often are guilty of asking for the blessing while missing what God is already doing. God knew that Daddy needed someone. He's not the most verbally kind and gracious person, but I believe he appreciates Ivy's coming into his life. Daddy always will have a complaint, and God always will provide.

Exodus 20:12 records these words, "Honor your father and your mother, that your days may be long upon the land which the LORD your God is giving you." That verse of Scripture is a commandment, not an option. My mother taught us to honor our parents, but I wouldn't accept the *father* part of the verse. Daddy showed little or no respect to the people with whom he shared a primary residence. His disrespect of Momma was very clear to many people in Clinton, including his children. He often treated Momma's children as if we were of no value. When Momma died there was no one to force me to honor Daddy. So I chose not to honor him. I was wrong.

When Momma died, I struggled with the right and wrong of the way we treated Daddy. I started off right and was doing quite well until what I saw as disrespect from Daddy reappeared. This time Momma was not here to pull me back in line. In fact I believed that Momma was not here because of Daddy's actions, reactions, and interactions. My inner self saw this as my opportunity to get back at Daddy for the way he treated Momma during the many years that they were married, and especially for the last four months of her life.

To show honor is to acknowledge, respect, and obey. I learned that the meanings of these words could be manipulated by circumstances. In my case I decided to acknowledge that I respected Daddy's wishes by obeying his request to leave his house. This kept me for a short while, but the Holy Spirit in me would not let me be at peace with myself. Because such behavior was foreign to me, I struggled.

The call of God within me continued to bother me about the way I was disrespecting Daddy. There was no excusable explanation for my behavior. Regardless of how Daddy treated me I had no right to act as I did. My pride was high, and I wanted to be in charge of me. As a Christian such a choice was not mine to make. I apologized to Daddy, and I think both of us felt much better than before. At least I did.

Inner Changes

Although I am totally convinced that life happens as God desires, the first few years after Momma died were no picnic. Knowing that my mother died was a small detail in my life's portrait. Being motherless was the larger segment that framed each moment. When Momma died, I learned that I had a lot to learn about living and life.

Because I considered myself to be a young, educated, Black woman who could handle anything, my life never stopped. I had an academic paper due, and Momma's death did not stop me from finishing my schoolwork. One of my seminary professors confirmed my need to be dedicated to being in motion by her first conversation with me upon my return to school. The exchange was brief and to the point. As I walked into her office, the professor said, "Hi, Sherita. I was sorry to hear about your mother." After glancing at my hand and before I could respond, she continued, "Is that your paper?" I gave her the paper, thanked her for her concern, and walked away from the office. At that moment, I realized I needed something, but I couldn't identify what the *something* was.

With major international incidents breathing heavily in my daily grind at work, studying remained a necessary priority. I needed to study; doing so kept me grounded. I couldn't fail now. Not passing a class would destroy me in life and disappoint Momma in death. I had to stay focused on making a 4.0 grade point average. Anything less than an A would be totally unacceptable to me.

During this time I wanted and needed to reassure everyone else and myself that life was no different for me now than it was before Momma died. This façade was not to be. My life began to fall apart, and the more effort I put into putting my life's puzzle together, the more I found that many more pieces were missing. The worst fact was that I didn't even know where to search for what I needed.

To say I was falling apart does not adequately describe what was happening to me. My dilemma was indescribably devastating. Living was not my goal. My husband and children were dear to me. They were always there, right beside me, but they couldn't take away the deep hole inside of me that was growing so fast that I feared being swallowed by it.

The many changes in life and shifts in schedules were taking their toll on me. I began to experience difficulty in concentrating on almost everything. Nothing mattered. Everything mattered. The pressure of knowing that Momma was dead and Daddy was alive was killing me.

I began to experience a new kind of pain—headaches. I craved sleep that eluded me. My work schedule became more erratic: 5:00 A.M. – 6:00 P.M. I was externally tired, but survival was my reason for being, my sole purpose.

Then almost as if an alarm sounded, my survival didn't mean anything to me. Happy and peaceful living was what I craved, but my will to live was hidden from my ability to do so. The deep hole was growing deeper, and I needed help.

On the first anniversary of Momma's death, I went to Solomon's Island, Maryland, alone. I didn't think I could spend the day in the presence of others. In my hotel room, I read, prayed, and slept. I had survived the proverbial first year. What a roller coaster ride! Somehow, on March 23, 1992, I managed to write in my journal. Reading this years later makes me realize that I was more "out of it" than ever. But the words sounded good.

> *Today marks the 1st anniversary of Momma's death. Until a few days ago, for me, this was to be a day of solitary mourning; however, a conversation with Harry changed my outlook. I didn't like or understand his reasoning. His method seemed selfish, considering he could talk with his mother any day. He told me that now was the time to stand on what I preach to others. As I thought about what he said, each statement began to be clearer. During my weak moments I began to call on God and draw back into mental recall of scriptures. Strangely enough I read Isaiah 40. I realized that my human strength and/or imagined power would not pull me through, but GOD could and would. In fact God wants me to pull through. He wants me to depend on the power that I have received through Jesus Christ.*
>
> *Not only that, but Isaiah 43:16-21 kept "nagging" at me. Yes, God is the God of the Exodus, but the same God did not stop working miracles at the Exodus. If I trust God, I will be delivered from the pain that has been felt so often during the last year.*
>
> *Often I tell others how God teaches in the bad times of life. Well, God does! James 1:2-4 talks about the development of human Christian character. God used the last 12 months to develop my character. I have learned so much.*
>
> 1. *Life on earth eventually ends—sometimes quickly—even for the ones who mean a lot to me.*
> 2. *How I live will determine whether my passage is peaceful or tormented.*
> 3. *My children need to know that death will come to everyone.*
> 4. *My spouse loves me more than I ever could have imagined. His patience is indescribably strong. I thank God for sending me Harry.*

5. My children need a good mother. They need to know that their mother loves them. I need to be more patient with Shari and Matthew.
6. I learned to question my motives for spanking. By spanking, what do I teach Shari and Matthew? They probably think it's all right to be beaten physically as long as the beater thinks the positives outweigh the negatives.
7. My brothers and sisters mean so much to me. We need to EXPRESS our love instead of **thinking** it.
8. I've learned that I can't fix everything. Some things can be fixed/straightened out ONLY by God.
9. My temper has to be controlled where my paternal parent is concerned. My paternal parent has dismissed himself to that role, and it is my position to respect his decision.
10. Money means nothing when compared with family love and unity.
11. Giving of myself for others is nice, but I must take time for me—to replenish and rest and get rid of some of this excess weight.

Thank you, God, for granting me a good day. Momma, I hope you're proud. Your "strange" little girl is growing up—finally. I hope I will be as good a parent to my children as you were to me. Thanks! I love you.

My siblings and I did not talk to each other on the anniversary. As is our family custom we avoided each other, pretending that the day held no major significance for us.

Nothing mattered, and everything mattered. Events that once brought positive anticipation now caused physical pain and high anxiety. Church, work, and social activities just didn't fit the bill. Having been an early riser for as long as I could remember, I responded to each morning's arrival with an anguished, "Ugh! Not another one." Life's joy was gone.

In April 1992, I received my denomination's first ordination, the diaconal. The service was emotionally moving. I cried not only because of what I thought, but also for what I felt. The awesome responsibility of being a minister who would declare what I heard God speak was overwhelming. Yet I realized that my personal anxieties and insecurities were hindrances to my having an effective ministry. There was no way for me to carry out my ministerial duties in my messed-up state of mind. I needed help.

My earlier discussions about my mental state brought Harry's response of "Sherita, if you get your spiritual life straight, everything else will work out fine."

For me, getting my spiritual life straight also meant getting my mental and emotional lives straight; there was no dividing the three.

I always had been able to fake my way through life. For as long as I could remember, I was never destroyed by life's calamities. I had overcome the worst parts of my existence. The emotional and mental straightening-out phase would be a cakewalk, a cut-and-dried-to-the-point issue. The responsibility of pulling myself back together was mine and mine alone. I never considered the possibility of God's having a role in my healing. I declared that in two weeks I would be cured of this malady.

Two weeks later was the first week in May. To my surprise I was not cured. The sinking feeling of being swallowed by a deep hole was quite disturbing. Why couldn't I fix this situation? Hadn't I fixed everything else that was painful in my life? Hadn't I plugged all the leaks, and didn't I check them periodically to make sure that everything was sealed tightly?

I told Harry that life was becoming too much for me. He listened as I explained that if I didn't get help soon, he would come home and discover at least one dead body. However, somewhere, hidden very deeply, inside of me was a person who believed in the possibility of being happy. I longed for a twenty-four hour period of feeling good. The time had come for me to begin the healing journey. Having missed my self-imposed deadline of two weeks to wholeness, I clearly understood that solving this problem would require help from God's using another human being.

Where could I begin? Quickly, almost instantaneously, I remembered having read the page in Saturday's local newspaper that listed church services. One church's ad indicated that counseling was available at the church. Voila! Somewhere between Sunday and Tuesday I dialed that church's phone number. After the signal from the answering machine I spoke these words and declared, "My name is Gayle Dillard, and I need to talk with a counselor. Please call me on 868——."

The morning of May 20, 1992 began as any other Wednesday: praying, meditating, reading the Bible and other devotional material. After getting Shari and Matthew out to school and daycare, respectively, I began tidying the house and preparing dinner. Because of my noonday Bible Study class and the probability of being detained at church, I always tried to get as much housework done before leaving in the morning.

Shortly before 10:00 A.M. our telephone rang. When I answered, a soft female voice responded. The caller asked to speak with Gayle Dillard. I responded, "You have the wrong number."

She said, "I'm from Washington Pastoral Counseling Service, and I'm returning a call from Gayle Dillard."

I gasped, "Oh! I'm sorry! That's me! I'm so embarrassed! My husband and I are ministers and since I had to leave a message, and I didn't know who would get the message, I didn't want to use my real name. Gayle is my middle name, and Dillard is my mother's family name."

The caller assured me that I had not committed an unpardonable sin and then asked the reason for my calling. The embarrassment of not remembering the name I used and the horror of hearing a live voice responding to my message stunned me. Somehow I managed to say, "I need help. I need to talk with a counselor."

The response came quickly, perhaps in response to the sound of my voice breaking, "Why do you need to talk with a counselor?"

I froze. The boldness that allowed me to call earlier had disappeared. For a split second the only part that moved on my body were the tear ducts that forced water from my eyes. My silence soon reminded me that the lady was waiting for an answer from me. So I said, "I was raped, and I'm having flashbacks."

"I'm sorry. When were you raped?" she asked.

"A long time ago, but I can't get it out of my mind. I keep seeing it over and over."

The lady inquired, "Do you prefer to work with a man or a woman?"

"A woman please," I said in a voice that must not have been much louder than a whisper.

After asking about my personal safety, she kindly told me that someone would be in touch with me within a couple of days. That response was perfect. My real plan was to call for counseling, schedule an appointment that would occur a few days later, and kill myself before my first visit to the therapist. This was such an easy plan, and I wouldn't have to disgrace my family and myself any further. With a couple of days to spare, all I needed was a suicide plan that was guaranteed to work.

During the time between leaving the message and hearing a response, every negative experience of my life flashed before me. From being teased about having freckles and sandy hair and being fat, to remembering students who rejected me for being smart, to hearing Daddy say to Momma statements such as, "Where did you get *that* one?"

But the thoughts didn't stop there. I believed that a group of people at Union Bethel were hell-bent on destroying my marriage and me. I was tired of subjecting myself to their insults and pranks. Killing myself would confirm their claims of my not being "holy enough" to be Mrs. Harry L. Seawright. The idea of satisfying their suspicions should have been enough to make me change my plans, but it was not so.

Just thinking of being free from life was exhilarating. In less than one week, I would be dead. What a relief! I thought about my children, not that they would be motherless, as I, but that they would not have to tolerate a mother who could not give them the kind of love they needed so badly. My thoughts about Harry focused on his not having to worry about my saying the wrong thing at the wrong time to the wrong people. Harry would be free from concerning himself with my bumbling social graces, my inclination to be a loner, and my feelings of low self-worth. My suicide would be the solution to all of my problems. This time I would succeed. Failure would not be smart enough to interrupt my plans this time.

As the morning continued, I hung up the phone in the bedroom and headed for the kitchen. Just as I was passing the bathroom, the phone rang. On the line was a very soft-spoken voice that said, "Hello, may I speak to Sherita Seawright?"

"This is she."

"My name is Carol Jacobsby (not the therapist's real name). I'm responding to your request for a counselor from Washington Pastoral Counseling Service."

"Boy! That was quick!"

"Excuse me?"

"The lady I spoke with said that someone would be in touch with me within a couple of days. I just hung up the phone from talking with her."

"I can see you at 1:30 this afternoon."

"Today? I have something to do from 12 to 1. I doubt that I can make it today. Where is your office?"

"It's at [the] Lutheran Church in Fort Washington."

"How much will it cost? I'm not working…"

"There's no charge for the first visit, and we'll discuss that when you get here."

"Let me check something out, and if I can't make it, I'll call you back."

She gave me directions and a phone number. I don't remember whether Harry was home, but I do remember talking with him. Believing that Harry was not serious about my being in therapy, I was surprised when he behaved as if he would not let anything, including my teaching Bible Study, be an obstacle to therapy. He offered to stay at the church just in case I needed to leave before completing the lesson.

Harry asked, "Do you want me to go with you?"

"No, I've got to do this one by myself. Maybe you can go another time."

What was wrong? Something had to be wrong! Every aspect of my life was working out for me to go to therapy on the same day that I received a response from my initial inquiry. My heart raced. I cried tears of fear and confusion. I couldn't go to therapy. Showing up would blow my image. What if this Carol person knew me? Why was Harry so cooperative? Was this a setup?

After completing my morning ritual of watching my favorite 1960s sitcoms, I went to meet the faithful folks who gathered for the noon Bible Study. We sang and prayed and studied. At 1:10 P.M., I was finished. I stopped at Harry's office to let him know that I was on my way. Again, to my surprise, he offered to go with me. I gracefully declined.

As I drove from the church's driveway, my thoughts were many and none. My life was about to make a serious change. In fact, having the nerve to make an appointment and proceeding to fulfill the same were major steps. Of the direction of the step—good or bad—I wasn't sure. Floral Park Road seemed to never end. The more I drove, the longer the distance seemed. As I tried to convince myself that I'd never get there on time, my adrenaline wouldn't relent. This must have been the day for me to begin taking care of me.

The Lutheran Church could easily be seen from Indian Head Highway, but getting there was not so easy for a trip packed with such nervous anticipation. I drove into the parking lot and followed Carol's instructions for getting into the building. She opened the door. As I walked into the "therapy room" I experienced what I know now was the Holy Spirit confirming in me that "today is the day, and this is the place."

Although I'm not sure what I expected, I am sure that my first meeting with Carol was not what I thought it would be. Not counting the days I spent in mandatory therapy as a Ford Fellow at Howard, my last official therapy session had been in 1980 in the psychology department at The Ohio State University. I remembered sitting, shaking, and crying as the student counselor talked with me.

Being in the room with Carol was different from the previous sessions in graduate school. I was in therapy because my life was at stake. In this room alone with a therapist who did not know me, I felt at ease. Since Carol was White, I didn't have to worry about seeing her at any gatherings of the African Methodist Episcopal (A.M.E.) Church. As far as I knew, she did not have a clue that my husband was pastor of a burgeoning church in Brandywine, Maryland. In this room and with this woman I realized that I could be me. There was no need for me to perform for others.

I examined my new surroundings. The room appeared to be divided by design. It was obvious that the space was used for other purposes. The therapeutic side of the area held simple furnishings—a sofa, desk, chair, table, and a box of facial tissue. The furniture was arranged so that I could look out of huge windows into the back yard with lots of green grass.

Carol explained what I called the rules of the therapy game. The only portion of a rule that stayed in my head was the one about confidentiality. She promised that our conversations would stay in that room unless one of the following happened: she sought my permission to release or audibly record information; she was ordered to testify in a court of law; or, if I threatened to hurt somebody else or myself. I accepted the disclaimer, completed and signed some paperwork, and began the journey that would change me forever.

Carol's first therapy statement caught me off guard. "Tell me about you."

Nobody had ever asked me to do such a simple act. In an instant, my response to Carol's statement found its way to my throat and stayed there. My chest began to burn, and I felt dizzy. Because I was Sherita Gayle Moon Seawright, also known as a strong Black woman, I wasn't prepared to let this woman, this stranger, intimidate me. As I fumbled to collect my thoughts and regain my composure without Carol's noticing, I asked, "What do you mean?"

"Well...what was life like when you were growing up? Tell me about you, your family, your goals."

The following is a taste of my response: I am thirty-three years old. I am the second child of four, the oldest girl. I'm married to an A.M.E. minister. I have two children, one girl and one boy. I am a student at Howard University School of Divinity. I was born in South Carolina and started going to school at four, although I didn't enroll until I was six. I explained my mother's occupation, told her about my aunt who cared deeply for me, and of how badly I miss my grandmother. I continued with information that I was always an excellent student, skipped tenth grade, graduated *summa cum laude* from Benedict, and earned my master's on a Minority Fellowship from The Ohio State University. I received a doctoral fellowship from the University of South Carolina but quit after two weeks, moved back home, worked as a substitute teacher, was hired by my college alma mater, and worked at Benedict until I moved to Maryland after getting married in 1982.

Carol did not interrupt me. When I finished, she nodded and quietly asked, "Was your father in the home?"

"What?!"

"Did your father live with you when you were growing up?"

"Yes."

"Oh, you didn't mention him."

With that the session was over, and I scheduled the next appointment for the same time, the same place, the next week.

The days passed quickly in a slow kind of way. I never entertained the idea of not going back to therapy, but there was no rush to spill my guts. I knew that the pieces of my personal struggle were gathered at the starting gate and the gun was raised and ready to be fired.

I quickly discovered that Wednesdays were days of wrath. Carol's questions and responses left little time for me to come up with what I believed were appropriate answers. The need to express myself was greater than I ever expected. Prior to therapy I was always removed from my feelings, but this talking process forced me to think and feel. In some ways therapy was the most trying time I ever experienced. I constantly reminded myself that the pain I experienced in the fifty-minute hour was not as physically difficult as the moments described. The hardest part of the ordeal was staying in the room with Carol instead of running away. There were many times when I wanted to cry, but, as usual, I forced the tears back to a familiar place.

My journal entry for May 27, 1992, the first day of real therapy shows

> *After the description [of the rape] I was asked how I felt. To be honest, such a question eluded me. I hadn't felt in so long. It was impossible to describe feelings for anyone, except Harry, Shari, and Matthew. But feelings, genuine feelings, are not a part of my life. I don't feel; it's not easy to explain, but what seems so normal to others is so difficult for me. It will get easier.*
>
> *I was asked whether I've ever wanted to die: "Yes"; whether I ever attempted to take my life: "Yes"; how many times: "2"; could I promise not to try again: "Yes, without a doubt." After my last attempt I promised God that I only would try again if I had a gun. Thank Jesus I am afraid of guns [now]. ...*
>
> *So I go forth, not living in the past, but trying to enjoy the present in spite of the past. God is still blessing me; I know the best **will** come. It is comforting to know that God knows (already) more than I ever will figure out by myself.*
>
> *These flashbacks are difficult, but not impossible. Of course, with God, I **will** prevail MIGHTILY! ...if for no other reason than greater is the one who is within me than the one who is in the world.*

My getting better was at a distance that was so far away that I could not see it. Almost immediately after telling Carol that I would not try to kill myself, I didn't want to live. She gave me the ultimatum of my telling Harry by a specified time or she would tell him. I told Harry, but since I didn't let Carol know soon enough, when I called her, she already had called Harry. This lady was serious, and I could not understand why. What difference did my life make to her? I was miserable, and there was no need for me to hang around any longer pretending to be living.

Carol was thorough. Why did she care about my mental state? She suggested that I make an appointment for a psychiatric evaluation. I fought the idea. My heart knew that she was offering her best, but her best would reveal the worst for me, and I would not participate in this plan.

Where could I go? My insurance plan was too risky. With the way my life had been moving recently, I would end up with a shrink who knew me, and that wouldn't work. Harry agreed with me, and inquired about sending me to the West Coast for the evaluation. Carol's task was to find the right psychiatrist. My task was to stay alive.

After a couple of days, Carol called with the doctor's phone number. This psychiatrist was one of the best in the field of mental health. She agreed to see me under terms that would prevent my records from being in a major mental health system's files. I agreed to go.

Harry drove me to the appointment. I was more afraid of going to the psychiatrist than I was of committing suicide. After an extremely short wait, Harry and I were invited into the office. With the introductions completed, the doctor, Harry, and I talked—she and Harry talked more than I did. Then she calmly asked Harry to leave the room. I wanted to leave with him, but I had come too far. Too many people had made too many sacrificial adjustments to make this visit possible. To leave now would be an act of ingratitude. I stayed.

After one and a half hours, Harry was invited back into the room, and the diagnosis was given. We were silent, but I don't think we were really shocked. Carol's suspicions of a kind of dissociative disorder had been confirmed. Harry was very gracious, but I saw the hurt in his eyes. He paid the fee, and we left. On the way home we talked a little. Carol was to have been notified before my next session with her.

I was terrified. Harry pledged his unfailing support. The "for better or worse" of our marriage vows was about to be tested in a way that neither of us could have imagined or understood. Our life was different, and, on that evening, so many things, events, and phases were made clear to both of us. Things that happened from childhood to college, graduate school, and marriage suddenly made sense to me. Neither of us appreciated what we faced, but we were determined to face it together, not knowing how difficult this would be.

Therapy was a bear of a task. I didn't want to go, but I was afraid to stay away. I watched my every move, kept records of my comings and goings, paid special attention to my behavior at work and at home. I stopped attending many gatherings that just a short time ago had been so dear to my existence as a student, minister, and pastor's wife.

Personal survival without losing my husband and children was my top priority and, to some degree, my only priority. I promised myself that everything was going to be fine before the summer ended. Again, I guaranteed my success. By the end of the summer I'd be cured, healed, and ready to resume my life at breakneck speed and pinpoint accuracy. My timeframe was wrong again.

Therapy continued to be on my weekly agenda. Carol and I spent many hours working through the mire and muck of my mental health. Each visit with her was a challenge. I never backed away, and, except for vacations, I never missed a session. We worked through many facets of my life. I learned how to talk and share a genuine smile. And then it happened.

On a particular Wednesday in late March, my appointment went as usual. When the session was completed, Carol told me that we needed to talk. The tone of her voice indicated that something terrible was about to happen to me. Carol informed me that she would be leaving the area almost immediately. As a nun who was completing her Ph.D., she was being sent to Europe. She knew this was on her schedule, but the timing had taken her by surprise. I asked how long she had known about this assignment. My heart sank with the news that she was privy to this information when we met almost a year earlier. She assured me that she had found a therapist for me. We would meet together the following week. I was crushed. She told me we needed to bring closure to our time together.

I explained that I needed no closure; I would be fine, but I felt used and abused by her. I was angry and not about to make her think that I couldn't go on without her. The words were not true. I did not want Carol to leave. She held personal information about me that I had shared with nobody else. To save face, I told her that all was well with me, and I hoped she enjoyed her time abroad. Before parting we agreed on the time and place of our meeting with the new therapist.

Carol's news was a powerful blow to me! Almost one month's time was left before my graduation from Howard. This was too much stress! Upon arriving at home, Harry greeted me with the usual question of, "How did it go?"

"Horrible. Carol's leaving" was my response.

"I knew that," he said.

"When did you find out?"

"She told me when I first met her. That's good; you haven't had time to get attached to her."

I resigned with, "Yeah, that's right." I wanted to cry, but I didn't.

By Saturday morning, I couldn't believe that Carol was leaving. Before we parted on the previous Wednesday, she gave me a telephone number where she could be reached just in case I wanted to clear up any matters that I faced. I called her and she agreed to meet me the following Monday in Greenbelt at the usual place.

I said my apologies for blasting her a few days earlier. I told her that I felt robbed, raped, and abused by her. She apologized for not letting me know earlier that she would be leaving. We parted on good terms, wishing each other well. We still were scheduled to meet the new therapist two days later.

To say that I wasn't prepared for a new therapist is the understatement of the year. Carol met me at a large Presbyterian church in Greenbelt, Maryland. I thought she would be present for the session, but, after making the introductions, she left. My final memory of Carol is her closing the door as she left the room. "It's over," I thought, "Carol is no longer in my life."

I sat in the new therapy room in a new church with the new therapist. The date was April 7, 1993. Her name was Norma Trax, and she worked for Pastoral Counseling and Consultation Centers. I didn't like the idea of having a new therapist. I wanted to continue my sessions with Carol. I didn't want to tell this strange woman my life's story and have her dump me as Carol had done. My feelings would not be hurt again, especially by a therapist.

Immediately my passive-aggressive mode kicked into the relationship. I would protect myself from attachment. This therapist never would know me because I wouldn't let her. In setting the tone of our meetings, Norma did the administrative thing. *Just like Carol,* I thought. She explained that she would not be at this location for long. She would be moving to an office downtown. That was all right with me. Since I wouldn't be her client for long, where she practiced mental health therapy was of no interest to me.

I clearly explained that I would come to therapy for a few weeks. Then I would graduate from divinity school and take some time for me. Therapy would not be on my agenda, but I promised to contact her after my hiatus. To ease my transition and to give Norma something to study while I was away, I wrote her a letter explaining my problem, giving skimpy information that seemed like details.

The ride back home offered me many minutes to consider this new phase of my life. *If God orchestrates my life, then this phase must be included in God's plan for me.* As I drove, I distinctly remembered an Old Testament lesson in the fifth chapter of Second Kings where a man was called to do a strange thing that also seemed disconnected from the desired results.

In the story, Naaman, a military commander, was sick. He wanted to be healed. As the prescription for healing, Elisha, a man of God, sent a message to Naaman telling him to dip himself in the Jordan River seven times. Naaman was insulted by the terms of Elisha's instructions, but even with hesitant obedience, Naaman was healed.

I don't know why that Scripture came to my mind, but I couldn't shake the lesson. The more I tried to forget the story of Naaman, the deeper it dug into my conscience. Was this a proverbial sign? If so, this was not what I wanted. There must have been another way for me to get healed without starting over with another therapist. I would use the next few days to find that other way.

On the Wednesday of the following week, I returned to Norma's office. She did not mention my previously unsolicited notice of taking a few weeks off from therapy. We began very, very slowly. I had to repeat some of the information that I had told Carol. This was my greatest fear. Saying the words and telling the stories again were almost as painful as when I talked with Carol, but just as before, nothing catastrophic happened. The session ended, and I was still breathing.

Going against my original plan, the following weeks found me going to therapy. I graduated from Howard Divinity School, sharing the highest grade point average of Master of Divinity students with my best friend. The final days of classes, papers, and preparation were interwoven with therapy sessions. God blessed me, and I survived the rigors of it all.

With graduation behind me, the summer before me, and no immediate employment opportunities, I focused on what was important—getting mentally fit. My children were to spend the summer in South Carolina, and Harry would be attending denominational and business meetings. Nothing else was more important to me than my getting well. The action plan was set, and I was going forward in pursuit of perfect mental health.

The summer was scary. I was afraid to be alone and more afraid to be with others. Yes, I was afraid that people would find out about my having a therapist. Although this fact was embarrassing, keeping the secret was worse than anything else I faced. My fear was with and without grounds for concern. With such uncertainty and my knowing that being around people constantly was a big part of my life, I drifted into a state of panic.

As my birthday approached, my attitude changed. I wanted to go away from everyone. I wasn't sure that I wanted to die, but living did not hold the thrill that was so pervasive just a few days earlier. Each moment seemed to drag. I didn't want to get up in the morning. I couldn't sleep at night. At other times, I only wanted to sleep.

Suddenly, everything shifted...again. Sleep and movement sustained me. As long as I could drive my car, I could survive. When I wasn't driving, I wanted to sleep. The fact of the matter was that being continuously active and settling for restless sleep caused me to be weary.

As I tried to get a grip on my behavior, I remembered that for as long as I could remember myself, movement was my key to survival. I couldn't recall sitting still for long periods of time. I was either walking around or in and out of a room or fidgeting in my chair or bed. I always read and wrote. My happiest days were spent with books, pencils, or crayons. Just walking through a store's stationery section brought me a natural high. Honestly, I could do many things simultaneously without experiencing distress. Hours of simply practicing my manuscript and cursive letters allowed me to be overtaken by serenity. I enjoyed reading the dictionary and remembered that when Midway Elementary School got a library and librarian in my fourth grade year, I knew that I would be at home as a library helper. Reading, writing, and physically moving allowed me to run from the pain of childhood. Now, here at the ripe old age of thirty-four, I was still running.

My weekly sessions with Norma continued. Living with mental pain was much more than I thought I could handle. As much as I hated therapy, I was afraid to stop. Retrospectively I know that God gave me the strength to go each week.

In August of 1993 Norma suggested that I visit a psychiatrist. My protests were laced with threats of "I'm not going through that again! I trusted Carol's advice and look what *she* did to me—she listened to my darkest secrets, and then she left me, just like every-body else." Norma made no promises except for her continuing to be my therapist if I chose to continue being her client. I liked her willingness not to make promises that she couldn't keep. I was struck most of all by her non-pushy disposition.

The psychiatrist discussion continued after my summer vacation. When Harry and I returned to Maryland in August, our children were with us. Life had to continue. I had to shift my focus again. During vacation I learned that I would start a new job in September. With little time left to get everything back to its perfect state, I began to panic. Suddenly everything seemed right, and I celebrated my health. But, just as quickly as every-thing had been made perfect, the bottom fell out of my life.

Norma was not available one weekend when I entered a cri-sis. Although she left a number for another therapist, I was determined not to include another person in this drama. The decision became bigger than I. On a Saturday afternoon in September 1993 I realized that my life was not getting any bet-ter. I wanted to die. I had one social obligation, and that would be my last performance. I am convinced that on that day God's Spirit took control of me and allowed me to dial the phone number to Adele Pogue, the on-call therapist. She sounded shocked to hear from me, but, in my usual form, since I had dialed the number, I would not hang up the phone without talking to her.

Adele listened very carefully to my verbal confusion. When I finished talking, she asked me to listen to her without inter-rupting. Adele told me that she heard my reasons for not getting psychiatric assistance. However, she wanted me to understand that if I was depressed it was not my fault. She compared depression to diabetes by saying that something happens in our body, and food and messages are not processed as in the past, but it's not our fault. However, just as I wouldn't blame a diabetic for taking insulin, I shouldn't blame myself for trying to find out whether I needed medication. This story was so simple it actu-ally made sense. I hung up the phone with a new determination to get more help. Norma made the recommendation, and I made the appointment.

In the book of First Corinthians, the Apostle Paul declares that planting and watering are in keeping with our Christian activities, but only God can give the increase. On that day in September, God allowed Adele to water what Norma Trax and Carol Jacobsby had planted earlier. Although I believed that I needed to see a psychiatrist, pride, fear, and rebellion stood between my healing from the depression that was eating my mental flesh and me.

Just as was the case on the day that I met Carol, my first visit to the psychiatrist was a *kairos* (Godly timed) moment. Entering the doctor's office, I was scared to go inside and scared not to do the same. As I sat down and examined my surroundings, my anxiety did not go away. In many ways my spirit was unsettled. I attributed my emotions to my having accepted the negative stigma that society placed on mental illness.

My mind raced back to the time when, as a fourteen-year-old, I told Momma that I needed to see a psychiatrist. She gently asked me, "What would people would think?" if they found out that the teacher's daughter was crazy. She meant no harm; yet, nearly twenty-one years would pass before I could get beyond her words and try to reach the place where I needed and wanted so badly to be. I decided that this visit to the doctor was for my husband, my children, and, most of all, me.

I made my intentions very clear. I had a therapist, and I wasn't interested in getting a new one. I was in this office to get medication. The psychiatrist assured me that he would be faithful to his professional ethics and would do whatever was necessary to accurately prescribe or alter medication.

In spite of my disbelief, the medication worked. Within one month of taking Paxil, I honestly felt better. I was able to think clearly. On most days, I didn't object to waking up in the morning; in fact, I began to look forward to each new day. Life became better and bigger: the more Paxil I took, the better my mental state became and the bigger my body grew.

My next visit to the psychiatrist resulted in a good report. Except for the extreme weight gain, the Paxil was doing its job. However, I could not afford to continue to grow in size. The doctor offered me an opportunity to try a new medication, and I gratefully accepted his offer.

Prozac became my drug of choice. Because this seemed to be the popular antidepressant of the day, I did not want to take it. Taking this drug would make me just like every other mentally ill person, and being just like everybody else was not my desire. In my reluctance, I could not escape the reality that I was feeling better than I had felt for most of my life. The risk was worth taking.

No, I don't like taking the medicine, but I also don't like feeling like Death's playmate. I often remind myself that the medication continues to help me just as insulin helps a diabetic. I face each day with happy anticipation. Yes, there have been times when I followed my urge to skip the daily dosage for a few days or weeks, but I had to return to the prescription. Faith convinces me that I will be free from Prozac soon.

My therapy continued for the next two years. Each week I went to therapy. Norma and I worked long and hard. One day Norma told me that she was praying that God would work a miracle in my life and bring total healing. I was shocked. She wasn't of the religious profession; so I inquired about her praying. She told me that she always prays for her clients. She wasn't asking me to pray, and I wasn't requesting that she stop praying.

Not only were Harry and I praying for me, but also my therapist was praying for me! This was a reinforcement of the scriptures that mentioned the presence of angels. I had noticed Norma's calm spirit, but her revelation made me think that God was using more people than I knew. Therapy remained an uphill journey, but I was convinced that God had ordained the order of my healing.

What did I learn in therapy? I learned that God made me on purpose and that, in God's eyes, I was not a mistake. I could not use my interpretation of anybody's rejection of me as an excuse for being rude, unconcerned, and mean to others. I learned that my past did not have to control my future, but it could become a divine catalyst to make me better. I had to release the pain of the past so that I could appreciate the joy of the present.

I also learned that I am responsible for how I live. Every day I have to make the choice to live. Nobody can or will live for me except me. God made me as one reflection of the Divine Creator's image. I must choose to be happy for me. Doing so frees me to share my happiness with others.

The most important thing I learned was to appreciate myself. Through therapy, prayer, and keeping a journal, I "met me" in a way that I never dreamed was possible. Before my experience in therapy, I thought that everybody who was not in touch with self was looking for an excuse for some area of life. After going through extensive therapy, I realized that we live in a society that is so synthetic that many people become someone else just to keep from being different from everybody else.

In therapy I learned to live the true meaning of Psalm 139:13-16.

> *For You formed my inward parts;*
> *You covered me in my mother's womb.*
> *I will praise You, for I am fearfully*
> *　　and wonderfully made.*
> *Marvelous are your works,*
> *And that my soul knows very well.*
> *My frame was not hidden from You,*
> *When I was made in secret,*
> *And skillfully wrought in the lowest*
> *　　parts of the earth.*
> *Your eyes saw my substance, being*
> *yet unformed.*
> *And in Your book they all were*
> *　　written,*
> *The days fashioned for me,*
> *When as yet there were none of them.*

This scripture continues to give me the strength to be me. Before therapy, I was me, but in a strange way. I was not willing to risk security for belief without being driven for negative reasons such as being rejected or misunderstood. After therapy, I became convinced beyond the slightest doubt that I am special in God's eyes. I had to acknowledge that I did want to be loved by others. However, if no human being chose to show love to me, I was capable of loving myself.

In making sure that I loved myself, I discovered that others began to show love to me in return. I admitted that maybe people loved me all the time, and because of my fear of being hurt, I refused to acknowledge or accept their love. In therapy I learned that genuine love demands that people be in relationship with one another. God made us so.

The mental therapeutic exercise taught me that I am not in charge of the world. If I take a nap, the world probably will continue to function without skipping a beat. I do not have the power to make *anybody* do *anything*. I'd heard this message in church all of my life, but I learned that God knows what I need and will provide my needs even when I don't know for what to ask.

Therapy taught me how to ask for help. After being a strong, independent, Black girl and, then, woman, I had convinced myself that I didn't need people. I was wrong. If I were going to be a healthy woman, I needed to learn to ask for what I needed and believe that other people would be mature enough to accept or refuse to help. I learned that, for the most part, other people's refusal to respond to my requests in the way that I desired was not a rejection of me. It was a personal choice on which my life did not depend. I can survive other people's "No."

Therapy was the vehicle that God made available to me. This might not work for everybody. In order to benefit from therapy, the client needs to have a mind for healing and a belief that God is able to heal by means that might be conventionally unacceptable in some religious settings. As a result of my experience, I am convinced that God uses all persons who make themselves available to be used. I understand that *therapy*, *therapist*, and *counselor* are positive words. Just because a mental health agent does not have the word *spiritual* or *Christian* on their business card does not mean that they do not have a relationship with God or that they are unable to help others heal.

I was blessed to have a husband who loved me enough to walk the journey with me. There were days when the therapy was a tremendous barrier in our relationship, but we endured. I learned that my husband really loves me. He stayed with me at times when I wanted to walk away from myself. Although family support is not a prerequisite for therapy, it does make the journey easier. Therapy is foremost for the person who meets with the therapist, but the persons in their life who can endure the struggle, will experience the pain and reap the rewards with the client.

Some of the people who knew me before I began therapy have asked if the therapy was worth the hassle. My answer is, "Yes!" But if I had known, in advance, the pain and agony of the process, I would have refused treatment. Now, as I stand on this side of therapy being happy, complete, content, healed, and relatively sane, there was no other choice for me. The new joy of being mentally healthy was worth the agony of therapy.

In Luke 13:6-9, Jesus told a story about a fig tree.

> *He also spoke this parable: "A certain man had a fig tree planted in his vineyard, and he came seeking fruit on it and found none. Then he said to the keeper of his vineyard, 'Look, for three years I have come seeking fruit on this fig tree and find none. Cut it down; why does it use up the ground?' But he answered and said to him, 'Sir, let it alone this year, until I dig around it and fertilize it. And if it bears fruit, well. But if not, after that you can cut it down."*

In this parable I always noticed the man's willingness to cut down the tree and the gardener's request that the tree not be cut down at that time. I missed the implications of the man's promise to "dig around" and "fertilize" the tree.

Before going to therapy I wanted to cut down my personal life. In a quiet voice, God spoke to my spirit and asked me to hold onto what was left of me. Now I know that therapy served as the digging around and fertilization processes. Though extremely painful and horribly smelly, both processes were necessary for me to bear good fruit. Hallelujah! Praise the Lord! I weathered the storm of therapy that brought me face-to-face with my past so that I could embrace the future. If Momma had not died, I probably never would have realized how badly I needed help. I probably would have died from a self-inflicted assault. Therapy and the professionals who offer their mental health services should not be bad words or forbidden fruit for Christians. God uses anyone who is available to be used.

Don't allow a bad experience with one mental health professional or other persons' opinions prevent you from seeking help that you believe you need. If you don't seek help, you'll probably always have a mental block for help, just as I had when Momma died.

Forgiveness

Forgiveness is a three-syllable word and a major force. I believe that many people accept forgiveness as something that must be done for them *by others*. However in Jesus' model prayer in Matthew 6:12, we are challenged to be forgiving people. At the end of the prayer, verses 14 and 15 go a step further by telling the reader:

> For **if you** forgive men their trespasses, your heavenly Father will also forgive you. But **if you** do not forgive men their trespasses, neither will your Father forgive your trespasses (emphasis mine).

The generic *men* in these verses applies to humankind. The ultimate interpretation is that God will forgive us in the same manner in which we forgive others.

Having read the Bible, in general, and this passage, specifically, I was convinced that I was in perfect agreement and good standing in terms of forgiveness. When Momma died, I realized that I was not as content in this area with myself as I thought I was. Looking back on the phases of my life from childhood to adulthood, I continuously saw examples of people who were unwilling to forgive. In the aftermath of many incidents, I saw that my biological family did not talk to certain people. There were some folks who I learned were invisible; their physical frames were present, but they were ignored and treated as if they didn't exist. Perhaps this response provided a survival mechanism. The sad part is that even though I noticed what was going on, I did not see a problem with the behavior patterns that I saw. For my family of birth, ignoring the parts of our world that offended us was the norm. This was my reality, and it was perfect.

When I left the confines of home to go to college, I soon learned that other families lived a lot differently from my family. I saw students whose families hugged and shared and actually missed each other when they weren't together. On the other hand my birth family taught me to keep a stiff upper lip. My siblings and I were taught "what happens in this house stays in this house." Years later, I understood the silent mandate, but the forgiveness piece was another matter.

In the early 1980s, my paternal grandparents separated. I do not remember a time when Granddaddy and Sook (our name for our daddy's mother) slept in the same room. Considering that my continuous interaction with them was limited prior to Granny's death, I never wondered about their living arrangements. I had seen them share meals at the round table in the kitchen and sit on their front porch. I have one memory of their being in the same car.

This marital split was quite interesting to me. I was home for a quarter break from graduate school when Daddy was called to the Big House (his childhood home) to help mediate a family dispute. This happened several times within one or two days. I clearly remember Daddy's coming home one evening and saying, in essence, that he was finished: he wasn't going back there again.

Daddy made that declaration on June 14, 1980. For the most part, Daddy kept his word. He neither changed his traffic pattern to avoid driving past his parents' house, nor dismissed his siblings who contacted him, nor prevented us from visiting our grandparents. Daddy chose not to visit his parents unless he wanted to, and, if he did, he never told us. He did not explain the reasoning for his behavior; he just reminded us that he told us he wasn't going back to their house.

I remember Sook's calling our house and asking my mother why Peter wouldn't talk to her. She could not remember having done anything to him that would make him turn against her. The hurt in her voice was obvious; her soft tone was filled with concern because of her youngest son's broken relationship with her.

Knowing that my relationship with my mother was strange, I still could not imagine not talking to her. Yet, my father's behavior seemed relatively normal to him and to us. In a small town, secrets are hard to keep, but I think Daddy was at ease with whatever people might have wondered or whispered. The situation never changed.

My paternal grandmother died on January 5, 1987. I was expecting our second child within two weeks. I knew that I would not attend the funeral in South Carolina, but upon receiving the news, one of my first thoughts was of my daddy. What would he do? Would his mother's death affect him? Would he attend the funeral? My mother wouldn't attend; she would be with me waiting for the grandchild. Would my siblings attend?

I'm not sure whether Daddy went to Sook's funeral. I saw a picture of him standing by the casket viewing his mother's body. His facial expression revealed neither overwhelming grief nor elation; he seemed to be at just another funeral. I never mentioned the funeral to Daddy, and he never talked about it to me. I did continue to wonder how he could have ignored his parent, especially his mother. Daddy wasn't my most favorite person, but totally ignoring him was not in my plans.

Four years later, I understood how a child could behave as if their parent did not exist. When Momma died, emotional pain, stress, confusion, and negative attitudes and actions resulted in our family's disintegration. The proverbial glue that held our immediate family together melted at Momma's funeral. Her death gave all of us the opportunity to release years of anger towards Daddy. Our unacknowledged anger at God was manifested in our attacks toward the only parent we had and the only person who we thought should have cared about us.

I still have no acceptable explanation for my behavior towards Daddy. I do know one thing: my family has an incredible creed. Although unwritten, it is a mental and social code that seems to have more power than is contained in most signed agreements. In our family, if a family member misbehaves, other family members will not hesitate, for all intents and purposes, to activate excommunication, thereby removing the errant person from the branches of the family tree. The saddest part of the problem is that the person who is no longer accepted as a family member often has no idea of the specific circumstances that led to their being ostracized.

In my mind, after Daddy asked us to leave his house and called the police to make sure that we did so, he did not exist. I never spoke the words that he was dead, but for all intents and purposes, he was. He asked for it. His behavior, not mine, was the cause of the way I treated him. If he hadn't called the police, then I wouldn't have been forced to ignore him.

The joy of not forgiving is found in blaming others. Not forgiving allows the person who holds the grudge to bask in the glow of "what was done to me." The other person is the one who must be blamed for whatever happened. In this phase of life, to be effective, the victim mentality must reign. Choosing not to forgive is the easy way out, the way of the coward, the no-win choice of people who live in fear. The fear is born in a person's inability to stand up to the crowd, or face the wind. Since comfort often can be found in standing with the majority, not forgiving is the choice of the feeble.

Within a short time of not speaking to Daddy, I became very uncomfortable. My youngest sister teases me for always wanting things to work out right and fair. This was neither fair to me, nor right towards Daddy. I knew better. Momma would not have approved; in fact, she would have been completely disappointed and disgusted. But the Moon blood in me ran too deeply within my veins and my heart for me to change my ways. What could I do?

Regardless of my outward display, I was totally disgusted with myself for not forgiving Daddy. However, days would pass when my primary thoughts were trying to figure out ways to get back at Peter Moon. I knew my thoughts were not in line with Christian behavior; I also knew that I had to let Daddy know that he hurt me. But most of all, he needed to learn the lesson that I was just as tough as he was.

In my bold state, my emotional and physical selves were struggling to survive. I returned to my old habit of biting my fingernails. For me, planning and trying to beat Daddy at what I understood to be his own game was stressful and necessary. Concentrating on important matters was almost impossible. Every sermon that I preached was a struggle with my hypocrisy. I tried to eliminate the words *daddy* and *father* from my vocabulary. I refused to accept God as Father. Using inclusive language provided my way of overcoming this ordeal, and it worked—for a while.

In July 1993, I spoke the words of forgiveness to a few others and myself. However, my state of forgiveness did not last long. I hated the sound of anyone who reminded me that Peter Moon was my daddy. My visits to Clinton, South Carolina were spent with my brother and my aunts. I tried to convince myself that Daddy didn't matter. I failed miserably in my attempts.

By New Year's Day 1997, my head was spinning from unforgiveness. Momma had been dead for almost six years. Nothing in my birth family made sense to me. I had to forgive this Peter Moon person. Yes, I was mad, and I was hurt. He deserved not having me in his life, but I could no longer live as I was living.

My decision to honestly forgive Daddy was the best choice for me. When I began to sleep better at night, I knew the forgiveness was for real. My anger towards Daddy lost its position as my primary focus. I was able to live again, not concentrating on this man who had hurt me so badly. However, I soon discovered that speaking forgiveness is only the beginning.

As I forgave, I made a mental note to keep my distance from Daddy. I could forgive him, but I would not trust him enough to become vulnerable again. What good, if any, would come from my placing my neck on his emotional chopping block again? I would not volunteer to participate in another game of torture with Daddy.

True to form, God had other plans. I was not a willing participant, but God's power prevailed. Seven months later in August 1997, while visiting with family in South Carolina, everything changed. My journal entry for August 23, 1997 tells the story.

> [God] I know that you have my life completely planned. Yet today confused me.
>
> This morning we went to Clinton. Our first stop was at Aunt Bannah's. She was in her front yard wearing her good straw hat that must be at least 30 years old. As soon as she realized who we were, she pulled/led Harry and me to her front porch and told Shari, Matthew [and]…to stay away.
>
> Aunt Bannah proceeded to say that she has to do what God tells her to do…and God told her to tell me that I mustn't leave town without saying hello to my daddy. She continued with her story of how Granddaddy had another woman and other children… But Sook knew, and because she loved Jack Moon she never said a negative word about him [to her children].
>
> "Sherita, you've got to forgive. You might not forget, but you've got to forgive. How can you preach to other folks when you're not living right yourself?"
>
> Harry was saying, "That's right! That's right!" I thought to myself, "This is a set-up!" I was stunned, shocked, and FROZEN! What was this about? Why was Aunt Bannah on this soapbox today? She knew the real deal. [She continued…]
>
> "Now my brother wants to see his grandchildren. Take them to see their grandpa. If you don't want them to go there, I'll call him to come here. That's okay? Who's in charge here?"

"It seems that you are, Aunt Bannah," was my reply.

Have you ever been so surprised until you can't move? That's where I was. I was 2 years old again. The only thing I remembered to do was put [anointing] oil on my family. Harry wanted none, but the children and I were anointed. Anyway, while we went to visit a cousin, Aunt Bannah called Peter Moon.

Within 5 minutes of our arrival back at her [Aunt Bannah's] house, Peter Moon was there. Matthew was delirious with excitement. ...He [Daddy] didn't recognize Shari. Aunt Bannah invited him to come to the porch. He shook Harry's hand; they chatted awhile; then he looked at me and said, "How are you Sherita?" I said, "O.K., sir." He inquired about my hair and invited us to his house. I still was having great difficulty realizing what was happening.

Aunt Bannah invited P.M. to take the children to his house. ... I was almost willing to bet my life that this was a set-up. Shari, Matthew, ...and P.M. left. Within 10 minutes Harry and I were on the way to South Bell Circle.

Upon our arriving at the house, P.M. was riding a bicycle. He motioned for us to park in the driveway. Harry obliged and asked [me] if I was all right. I was. As we entered the house, P.M.'s wife—my stepmother, Ivy, greeted us in the living room. Her words were, "You must be Sherita. ..."

She is very nice. ... All during our stay, she thanked us for coming to see them and letting P.M. see the children.

As I sat on the porch, I kept thinking, "I must be dreaming." The porch contained many items that I remembered— the clock, the lovebirds, the exercise machine, the furniture, the see-through phone. The washer and dryer still were in place. The kitchen was the same.

When we were ready to leave I asked permission to look into the room where Momma died. Harry came through and asked if everything was all right. I said, "I just wanted to see where she died."

By now I "realized" that I was in the house of my birth. The amazing thing was that only a few things were different from my *last visit. There was a new sofa. The piano was in the living room. I don't remember seeing the dining room table. The fireplace was closed (with a wooden board). The kitchen still had the same appliances.*

In the midst of my leaving, I got a closer look at something that caught my eye earlier on the way to the sun porch. The piano is in the living room, and over the piano is a picture that was taken on Laurethia's college graduation day when we all gathered in front of the Learning Resources Center on Benedict's campus. The picture was in a beautiful frame. What really struck me was the size. The photo had been enlarged to at least 28 inches. This was the only picture I saw of us. I did not remember seeing a picture of Momma.

As I sat on the sun porch my heart realized that God reigns. P.M. is one miserable person. He can hardly hear. He looks worn down, beaten. His wife answers for him a lot. But P.M. is one miserable soul. ...

Today I saw a sermon... a sermon about sowing and reaping. Galatians 6:7-10 was the text. P.M. is reaping his harvest. Everything he talked about was "things." He bought more land, another house, a new shed; he's going to buy a new [car].

But God is sovereign! When we returned to Swansea, I asked Harry if the visit was a set-up. He said, "No, that was all Bannah!"

So...there you have it! Oh what a day...today is August 23, 1997. Mom has been dead exactly 6 years and 5 months.

That day, forgiveness took on another meaning for me. I never imagined being able to regain a part of my life that seemed to mean nothing from the beginning. I had spent a large part of the day with Daddy, the man who hurt me by hurting my momma, my siblings, and me. I recognized my father, the man who had such power when I was a child, but, in reality, I saw a different man.

The Daddy I grew up with was a proud man who wanted to put his best foot forward; now he seemed to stumble. The Daddy whom I knew as a child didn't seem to care about family;

now he was thrilled to be in the presence of his relatives, even me. This was a weird experience for me.

As I sat in Daddy's house that day in August, I reflected on my desire to get back at him. Prior to my considering forgiving Daddy, I wanted to make him pay for everything he had done to me, his family, and especially to Momma. However, on August 23 God showed me that I was not the one to repay. Yes, I'd read the scriptures in Deuteronomy 32:35 and Romans 12:19. I knew that I was not to repay evil for evil. However, the desire to do so was embedded in me deeply.

Ever since Momma died I spent many hours plotting, and planning, and dreaming. I never wanted nor intended to hurt Daddy physically, but, if he were capable of feeling hurt, I wanted him to suffer severe emotional pain. I wanted him to feel the abandonment from us that I was convinced Momma felt from him. Being in Daddy's presence that day made my life worth living. I saw what I recognized to be God's hand on Daddy's life. I could never have done the job as well as God was doing.

Looking at Daddy, his wife, and their surroundings, I felt something that reminded me that God's hand was on my life also. The mess, the arguments, the hatred, the resentment and all the other negative and mixed feelings I had experienced had come full circle. God made it clear to me that I was not perfect either. God was showing me that just as I thought God had changed Daddy through time, the same God used the same time to change me too.

Most of all, I understood that my change was not dependent on what God did to Daddy. God's change in me was a personal encounter that I needed to acknowledge and accept. I knew that genuine forgiveness was taking place. At that moment I learned that forgiveness is not an event, but a process, a process I was just beginning. I understood that forgiveness for me meant that I had to behave towards Daddy as God behaves towards me. Although I was convinced that I never could forgive as God forgives, I knew I had to try.

I slept that night, not in a deep sleep; too much had happened that I had not scheduled. Yet, I slept with a peace that had eluded me for years. I know God changed me that day. My heart went out to my daddy. He was no longer just my biological sperm donor; he was my daddy. For good or for evil, we belonged to each other, and neither of us could deny that fact. To be honest, I didn't want to deny him. I probably will never know what that day in August did to Daddy. I do know that it changed my way of living, and it changed me.

Forgiving Daddy had set me free. I no longer had to waste time focusing on the negative side of him. I allowed God to do what God wanted to do for so long—free me to live. Daddy didn't become a saint that particular day, but I no longer saw him as a man whom I needed to hate. I saw him as a man who needed his family's love and whose family needed his love in return. I knew that I would love him as best as I could. Yes, doing so would be a test, but I realized that it was only in my forgiving Daddy that God would forgive me.

So how is my Daddy-forgiveness level now? Since that time of my first visit, I have spent time with Daddy and my stepmother. Our son has spent part of his summer vacation with them. The relationship is not like "old times"; in some ways it's better. The old-time way was a fake, pretending to get along just for Momma's sake. This time is for real because I want and need to have a relationship with Daddy. I love my daddy, and I believe he loves me. We don't see eye-to-eye on many things. We don't talk to each other every week, but we do respect each other. As much as I hate to admit it, we are alike in many ways beyond the physical appearance.

One part of this forgiveness experience that I regret the most is that Momma cannot share this with us. Daddy and I probably would not have gotten to this level of understanding and relative appreciation for each other if Momma had not died first. My being able to forgive Daddy falls within the line of death's bringing life. Through Momma's death I learned to forgive. And now, because of forgiveness, I am learning to live.

The Next Level:
As a Wife

When Momma died, I had to accept the fact that life is uncertain. I had no other choice. The biological foundation of my existence had crumbled, and I was lost. But even in the midst of the uncertainty, I realized that a person would be wise to prepare for the future. Without making preparation for the future, individuals become *targets of* life rather than *participants in* life. I was not a stranger to preparation, but when Momma died, I had to shift my plans. I realized that life would never be the same for me. It was left to me to choose a course that was best for me.

Somewhere within a year of Momma's death, I realized that God really is awesome. I no longer only saw God as the awesome God of fear and dread, but I began to understand God to be the awesome God of faith and power. It became crystal clear to me that if I were to go forward, I would have to yield complete control of my life to God. Before Momma died, I was convinced that my spiritual surrender to Jesus was accomplished. With Momma's being gone I discovered that my spiritual self-assessment was inaccurate.

While in seminary at Howard, I enrolled in what was the most difficult, yet fulfilling, class of my tenure—Systematic Theology. Because of the strain of trying to understand the readings and discussions, I dreaded going to the class each week. I remember talking with the professor about my lack of confidence in comprehending the basic course material. He assured me that if I kept up with the readings I would be in good shape. I didn't want to be in *good shape*; I wanted and needed *excellent academic grades*.

As the weeks went on and I continued to read, I began to experience a deeper relationship with God. My faith began to increase, and the burden of grief began to show some signs of being lifted from my life. Studying for Systematic Theology forced me to think. While trying my best to read the assignments, I realized that God has many ways of revealing the divine to us.

Before Momma died, I was limited in my view of God. The God that I experienced and to whom I prayed was for people who had been saved, as I had, by repeating the sinner's prayer and asking God to forgive me of my sins and live within me. Only Christians were really saved.

It was while reading books for Systematic Theology that I began to think that God possibly could love non-Christians. Jesus talked about having "other sheep" that we do not know. Maybe, just maybe, to someone else, I, along with other Christians, was one of the "other sheep."

The biggest eye opener came in the form of a reading assignment that included the Apostle's Creed. As a dedicated member of the African Methodist Episcopal Church, I recited this creed each Sunday morning. However, the phrase, "I believe in… the communion of saints" previously held no major significance for me. With Momma's death and seminary studies, I saw the phrase in a new light.

I realized that each Sunday as I spoke the words, "I believe in … the communion of saints," I was saying that I believe I am in fellowship not only with saints, Christians, and believers who are alive today, but I also am in fellowship with saints, Christians, and believers who are not yet born and who have already died.

What a revelation! My not being able to physically be with Momma did not mean that my connection and relationship with her was totally gone. Jesus was our common bond. Not only was I in communion with Momma, but I also was in communion with Granny and Sook. What a way to go!

For those of you who will accuse me of non-Christian demonic practices, I am not promoting séances or ongoing conversations with the dead. My only claim is that in my thinking of what I recite as my faith conviction, I found solace for my grief. I found my relief in my faith. How strange! Or is it? Shouldn't our faith be able to sustain us in our lean times of struggle and loss just as in times of ease and gain?

As a Christian I was grounded in faith, or so I thought. However, it was not until Momma died that my faith had to work in a way and a degree as never before. Before Momma died, my faith in her was real. I always knew that Momma was there for me, for good or for ill, whether I liked it or not, to give me the encouragement or the painful prodding that made my life so interesting. To be honest, my faith in Momma took priority over my faith in God.

It was not until Momma died that I had to draw from a well of faith that had been in me all the time. Like so many people to whom I had ministered, I was not willing to let down my bucket to draw from the faith well. I always had Momma. When she was alive, her ways irritated me, partly because I couldn't understand our relationship. I couldn't figure out why Momma behaved as she did toward me while showing love. However, I never doubted the peace that I saw in her life, especially during her last years and days, and I never stopped loving her.

But when Momma was no longer with me physically, I had to learn to rely on God in ways that I never imagined. Momma and I often spent one to two hours on the phone each day. The time was not always continuous, but if we forgot to mention something, we just called each other back until we finished our conversation. When Momma died, not being able to talk with her on the telephone was a major adjustment, probably one of the most difficult. I wondered how I would use this extra time. Talking to my aunts wouldn't be good enough to fill the void. Each conversation with them, in a new kind of way, reminded me that they were my aunts, not my mother. They were consistent in their love, but because of Momma's being physically absent in my life, talking with my aunts was painful.

After arriving home from work one day, I was surprised by a reality and an idea that seemed so obvious: Momma and I never would experience another telephone conversation. However, the next revelation startled me: I could use that extra time to begin to develop a deeper relationship with God. God was my spiritual parent who not only knew what I felt, but also knew what I needed. In God's own time, I was being made aware of His presence and position in my life.

What a blessing! The many things and experiences that had occurred in the time since Momma died began to come together for me. Nothing changed externally, but on the inside of me, my spirit began to soar to another level. It was at that time that I saw and understood that the time had come for me to rise up and become the woman whom God had called me to be. My time was now! What would I do with it?

Although I don't remember the exact date, I do know that my post-Momma life changed that day. Now was the time for me to begin to live what I had been taught. My faith would now be seen in my works: my life with my husband, children, friends, and business and personal relationships. Living on this level would be a dramatic change for me, but I also knew that, with God's pulling for me and my staying in tune with God's Spirit, I could only go higher in Christ.

Many people are familiar with the Proverbs 31 wife. This woman must have been perfect. Thousands of years later, she is the subject of many women's group discussions. Next to the story of the Virgin Mary, the Proverbs 31 wife's story is probably one of the most lauded descriptions of a woman in the Bible. The passage is intriguing, but I confess that I do get tired of reading about her. Sometimes I think that women are too lazy to look for other examples of womanhood and, therefore, use the wife of Proverbs 31 as a default character.

After praying and seeking God's counsel, I was drawn to this much-used passage. Verses 10,11a, and 12 spoke volumes to me.

> *Who can find a virtuous wife? For her worth is far above rubies. The heart of her husband safely trusts her…She does him good and not evil all the days of her life.*

Was my mother a virtuous wife? Yes. Was her worth far more than rubies? Without a doubt. My question was: *How did she do it?*

Thinking and praying yielded the following plan. I would become a virtuous wife. My husband would be able to trust me, and I would do my husband good and not evil all the days of my life. Although I knew this would not be an easy task, I had no idea how difficult it would be.

Having watched my mother be what I interpreted as a "doormat" to my daddy, I was clear that I could not and would not be the same for Harry. I'd always had an opinion, and such would continue to be the case; however, I was willing and determined to learn to speak the truth in love. What better place to start than with my husband?

Although speaking had never been a problem for me, I also had a gift of being silent and ignoring people, a gift of environmentally genetic origins. So whenever Harry got on my nerves or did something that rubbed me the wrong way, I would shut down. I wouldn't complain, but my passive aggressive behavior would soar. When I decided to talk again, the venom would pour forth without mercy.

If I were to be a virtuous wife, this vicious cycle of processing people would have to stop. I would have to face my fears, speak up without threatening others, and learn to trust myself so that my husband would be able to trust me. I really would have to learn to love three people: me, myself, and I.

My first act of loving me was to begin seeing myself. I cut my hair, not just in a short style, but also in a short natural style with no chemicals. This act did not endear me to my husband or my children, but for me, cutting my hair made all the difference. Each day I would be forced to see myself, not the part of me that was peeping out from my hair, but the genuine me, with freckles and whatever else.

Soon I learned that people, many of them supporters of Black empowerment motifs and celebrants of African heritage, were very uncomfortable with my haircut. The fact that I was comfortable with my short natural was more than disconcerting to others. It seemed as if people wondered what pricked the nerve in me to commit such a brazen act of defiance!

Learning to love myself was not easy, but I was determined to succeed. I began to talk to myself about myself. In the morning I would take time to look myself straight in the eye and say, "I will praise you, O God, for I am fearfully and wonderfully made! Marvelous are Your works!" Those words were a key element of my acknowledging my God-given status of having worth.

In performing such a simple act, I began to believe what I said, and I began to enjoy this game. Perhaps the secrecy gave me power that I never had. Since nobody knew about my ritual of self-empowerment, I relished my private time with me. Speaking positive about me allowed me to *hear* positive things about me. Each day I wrote a positive word describing either how I felt or how I wanted to feel that day. As in Proverbs 18:21, I found death and life in the power of the tongue. The death was in relinquishing the negative view that I had of myself, and life was found in speaking the positive. I realized how special I was to God.

I asked God to help me appreciate me, not in a reactive way but in a proactive way. Being proactive would allow me to act before I received other people's vibes or responses. If God would just continue to guide me, I was willing to try to glorify God with my life. I committed myself to spending less time each day thinking about what I thought other people thought or said about me. This was genuine progress.

In time God blessed me to move from thinking about and trying to discern other people's thoughts. In my transition I developed a better relationship with God. My time in keeping a journal allowed me to write notes to God. These notes were so personal that I was ashamed of many of the scribbles. I didn't want to see them again, and since God knew what was on the notes, I ripped the papers to shreds.

Within a few months I noticed a change. In feeling good about myself, other people noticed as well. Harry was aware that *something* was amiss. As I changed, I believe that Harry wanted to praise me, but the intensity of my changing had a negative affect on our relationship. He was changing too, and both of us needed time to adjust. The adjustment period was very taxing. While our energies were focused on personal agendas, other people were focusing on destroying our marriage. After adding the pressures of Harry's being a pastor at a growing young adult church, the perfect recipe for disaster was in place.

Our marriage suffered for many reasons, but Harry and I usually were able to talk and pray. I began to understand that I was married to Harry. Consequently, according to God's word in Ephesians 5:22, God was holding me responsible for submitting to my own husband. If my marriage were to be solid, I would have to respect my husband above all other human beings. Allowing other people to set standards for how I lived with Harry would be out of the question.

Yes, we survived the threat to our marriage, and, yes, we carry the scars. For all the pain that we endured, our marriage is better. After looking back at all we went through, I believe that the ordeal was an answer to my prayer. It was during the difficult times of our marriage that I learned to trust only in God. I had nobody else to seek. Few people would have listened to my report, and those who listened would not have believed what I said.

During this time I learned how to pray, not simple prayers, but prayers from the deep recesses of my heart. I felt very safe and secure in pouring out my heart to God. I did so without complaint or restraint from God. I learned that tears are acceptable to God. As my tears were put in a bottle (Psalms 56:8) I learned that God really listens to me. Several times in my prayers I experienced God's presence in a way that made God seem physically with me.

God chastised me and showed me how I was wrong. I could no longer punish Harry for my childhood and my relationship with men. God clearly helped me to understand what I already knew: although Harry was not a part of my childhood, after hearing the story of my childhood, he loved me anyway. I began to realize that Harry was a gift from God to me. I began to look at the brighter side of the relationship, and I liked what I saw. In retrospect, I believe that telling Harry that I was trying to change might have helped him during my transition.

The real message to me was that I had changed. As I focused on the good and made rational, clearly thought-out decisions about the bad in me, I had begun the same process in my relationship with Harry. In seeing myself as my personal cheerleader, I realized that I was supposed to be Harry's cheerleader, too. I have accepted this challenge. Even as a former feminist/womanist I have no regrets in my decision to support Harry. Doing so has made my life more productive and less stressful.

In clearing the clutter from my life, God showed me that Harry was also cheering for me. God reminded me that Harry Seawright was busy the very first time I saw him. Before I got married, Momma told me she believed Harry was a good man, but she wanted me to understand that Harry would always be busy. His "busy-ness" had bothered me for quite some time, but now, I have begun to understand Harry's busy schedule as honoring his commitment to helping, not only our family, but others also.

For the first time I understood the responsibility and stress that Harry felt as the man of the house. He took his place in the family as a serious position. His focus was not on the title of "head of the household"; he accepted the ups and downs that accompanied the title. Harry explained that he had to live and work in a mindset that could survive my deciding not to return to work. It was through this process that I learned, understood, and accepted that Harry was my friend, not my enemy. He and I needed space to grow separately as individuals so that we could grow together as a couple.

My final analysis is that if I am a woman who aspires to be a virtuous wife, I have to stay focused on my marital vows to God and to Harry. I cannot allow outside forces to dictate how I live as a wife. By keeping in mind that I am married to one man, and knowing that he is the one and only human man who still brings me a special kind of joy and excitement, I only can go higher. I have to continue to trust Harry and know that he loves me as much as I love him.

On this phase of my journey, everything did not pan out as I would have hoped. Some of the experiences and hurdles that I thought would kill me actually worked for my good. Yet, other experiences that seemed positive really tore at the core of my soul and brought a negative result. I also made terrible mistakes that seemed to be extremely appropriate at the moment of decision. From my struggle with me, myself, and I developed a peace in my marriage relationship that is beyond my comprehension. Could this be a result of my being at peace with God and with myself? In retrospect, I know now that Momma had the same kind of peace.

So how did my Momma become a virtuous wife with a worth that was greater than my precious birthstone? I learned that it wasn't an easy way for her, but Momma was clear on at least two concepts. She married Peter Moon by choice, not chance; she stayed with him because she loved him. Regardless of what went on in their marriage or what others said about Daddy or how tough I believed staying with Daddy was,

Momma continuously relied on God, trusted herself to hear from God, and lived her life as she thought was best according to God's standards. In doing so, she lived the life of a virtuous woman and became a virtuous wife. So far, I believe that, in my own way, I am headed down the same road of respect.

In Proverbs 31:25 the messages are clear:

Strength and honor are her clothing;
She shall rejoice in time to come.

Strength and honor aren't garments that fit everybody. They can be worn only after a struggle. Military, sports, and academic citations are given after the battle. The decorations and diplomas are reminders not only of a victory, but also of a struggle.

I believe that it is in our times of struggling that we learn what lies deep inside of our hearts. In my quest to be a virtuous wife for my husband, God showed me a stronger part of myself. I discovered that spiritual part of me that held me together. Because of my struggle for self-improvement, I am convinced that I am a better person. My battle scars are healing, but I proudly wear my medals of strength and honor. As is the case with formal and informal education, no one is able to take away these hard-earned personal lessons.

After much is written about the Proverbs 31 lady, after the accolades, and after the report of her diligence, the final saluta-tion of verse 30 is:

…a woman who fears the Lord, she shall be praised.

I pray that I will always fear the Lord. I always want to live in gratitude to God for sending Jesus to die for me so that I could walk this journey knowing that I will spend eternity with Him. Fearing God allows me to continue to connect and commune with Momma. She feared the Lord. Because of this, many people, especially her four adult children, are still praising her. I count it a joy and a privilege to try to follow in her footsteps.

The Next Level:
As a Mother

Psalm 127:3 declares, "Behold, children are a heritage from the LORD." In my family of birth, children were little people who showed up at intervals. Shari Nicole, our firstborn, was my parents' first grandchild and the first baby in the immediate family in seventeen years. Harry Matthew, our last child, was born exactly twenty years after my youngest sister.

Mothering was not instinctive with me. I never babysat for other people. Being around small children was a foreign experience. When I married Harry I knew that children were in his life plan. He mentioned having eight children. I told him that would happen with his second wife. Then he wanted four. After two children and a thorough examination of our life's work, we both agreed that we probably had our hands full.

Our children are a blessing from God. The first miracle is in the fact that I do have children. Of the four siblings, I was probably the one voted "Least Likely to Procreate." No, I didn't hate children, but I was very career-oriented. When I was growing up, I saw that women who had children had little time for careers. My mother worked all day every day, came home, and worked some more. She cleaned, cooked, took care of us—thank God somebody else did the laundry—and did anything else that needed to be done. On the other hand, Daddy went to work, came home when he wanted to, and did nothing except what he wanted to do. I thought this was quite unfair and disrespectful. So, in order for me not to be in the same kind of mess, I would stay single, be a law professor, travel the world, and be childless and filthy rich. After meeting Harry and accepting that my plans were changing, I decided that *children* and *Sherita* could peacefully coexist.

I became pregnant in October of 1982, less than one year after getting married. Momma had been very excited about the pregnancy, thrilled beyond words. That pregnancy ended in a miscarriage. I was hurt. People's ignorance and their most insensitive remarks startled me: "You'll have another one." "You're still young; you can still have more." My silent and secret response was, "But what about *that* one? Doesn't *that* baby count?"

Momma told me to get a bottle of an old-time liquid vitamin. She described its potency by saying that every bottle contained a baby. I cannot dispute Momma's claim because two months later, I became pregnant. While the Moons were relatively silent, the Seawrights told everybody. Because of the recent miscarriage very early in the previous pregnancy, Momma wanted to be careful in spreading the news; she only told her sisters and my siblings.

The horrors of my first miscarriage were forwarded to future pregnancies. Every day that I was pregnant, I lived in the fear of having another miscarriage. I proceeded with every precaution. My mother-in-law was a tremendous help, as were some of people at the church where Harry served as pastor. The good news is that this baby was born healthy. We named her Shari Nicole.

Having a baby around the house was exciting. Shari's smiles and tears brought Harry and me to our knees. There was nothing too good for our baby. Since I chose to nurse Shari from my breasts, she was responsive to me out of necessity, but her heart belonged to her daddy.

After going through labor with Shari, I promised myself *never again*. This was it. Shari would be an only child. I enjoyed being home with Shari for six weeks, but work was on the horizon. One of our adopted mothers referred us to a great day care provider. Harry took Shari to the sitter every morning, and I brought her home in the afternoon. My heart was changing about work, but Dillard and Moon women were known for being self-supportive. I wasn't about to break the chain of employment and be forced to depend on a man to take care of me.

Just before Shari turned two, we enrolled her in a neighborhood private school. This simple change for her was a major change for me. I think it signaled that my little baby was growing up. Not long after her enrollment, something else started to happen—I felt a steady emotional gnawing at my womb.

My new feelings were not difficult to sort. I wanted another child. I think Harry was surprised to hear me say the words, but we decided to try to have another baby. After four months of trying to conceive, the results were negative. Since we weren't being successful in our quest to get pregnant, we decided: *Oh, well.*

At that time in the 1980s, the real estate market was booming. We decided to put our house, a bungalow in Northeast Washington, D.C., on the market just to see what would happen. What happened is that a buyer made an offer on the first day that the house was posted on the real estate listings. We were in a bind. We had to find a house.

The plan for another baby took a back seat to looking for a house that we could afford. The next few weeks brought the news that Harry was going to be assigned to another church. With all our energies concentrated in these areas, the unexpected happened: I became pregnant. The baby was scheduled to arrive on January 14, 1987. Harry and I were happy. Shari received the news with a smile; I am sure she didn't understand all the implications for her, but she was very clear that "there is a baby inside Mommy."

This second pregnancy was completely different from the first. With Shari, morning sickness ended precisely six months before she was born. With Matthew, I was sick every minute of every day of the entire pregnancy. The fact that I was expecting became undoubtedly obvious in my seventh month of pregnancy with Shari. Matthew's presence was known within two months of conception.

In spite of my anxious fears, we welcomed a feisty Harry Matthew into our family. He was very different. He constantly moved. When he awakened in the morning, we knew it immediately. There was no adjusting to the day. He awoke with ideas of how to make everybody's day more interesting.

Now, with two children, I was happy but still uncomfortable. How would I manage? My mothering information came from a good source, but I wanted a different kind of life for my children. My childhood was a setting where children were tolerated and love was dispensed with things. I wanted my children to experience genuine, emotionally tangible love. I wanted to give them things along with the knowledge that they were wanted and not a nuisance. I wanted to nurture their gifts and encourage them in what they wanted to do.

I tried not to get bogged down into trying to force my children to do the things that I wanted to do as a child but couldn't. However, there was one goal that meant a lot to me. Because my energy was focused on academics, I had plans of my children's excelling in school. Harry believed in children being allowed to be children. For him life provided learning, and the children would be educated in common sense and academics. I chose a different option. Structured academic learning was my drug, and I wanted our children to follow me in my addiction. I wanted my children to be smart, and since reading was the key for me, reading also would be the key for them.

Shari and Matthew are extremely smart children, but they learn in their own way. They are also very good teachers. They taught me that I couldn't make them learn. I can only present opportunities to learn and create a positive learning environment. This message was clear. I would have to find another niche.

Since I couldn't graft them into my world, I think I gave up. My premonitions had come true. I didn't have whatever was necessary to be a good mother. Our children became Harry's children. He knew how to play, have fun, and parent. I didn't have a clue about these things. I distanced myself from Shari and Matthew. I cooked meals and took care of the home after work, while Harry did church work. But those were Harry's children. He nurtured, loved, and showed them the good sides of life. He took them to carnivals and the mall. I took them sightseeing in the nation's capital, showing them the memorials, buildings, and the subway system. This unspoken arrangement didn't bother me immediately. However, eventually I longed for a closer relationship with both of my children.

God's plan to grant my longing began to unfold in the summer after Momma's death. As was the case with many graduate students, I needed money to stay in school. Earlier in my freshman year at Howard Divinity School, I applied for a Ford Foundation Fellowship. The more I tried not to think about the fellowship, the more my mind was consumed with the thought. I was working full-time, going to school full-time, serving as a ministerial licentiate and a minister's wife. The responsibilities of mothering claimed the time that was left.

After waiting for most of the summer, I finally was told by the program's director that I had been awarded a fellowship. There was one problem with the award: because of my high income, I could not have tuition remission. Upon my inquiry I was told that if I did not work, I would be eligible for the tuition grant. Since I believed so strongly in working, this was a grueling choice.

Realizing Momma had been dead less than six months, I didn't want to become guilty of post-traumatic stress behavior. I had heard about and witnessed people's making major life changes while in the throes of grief, only to find out later that their decision was impulsive, ill advised, and wrong.

Harry and I talked about my stopping work. For nine years, I was a government employee. I was making a comfortable living with a GS-12 salary and great benefits. This was a lot for me to forfeit. As we pondered the future, I knew we had to consult God about the matter, but I didn't want to do so. I was afraid that God would say, "Go for it!"

My gut reaction was to stop work, go to school full time, and accept the fellowship. My common sense reaction was to keep working, make more money, and stay secure while attending school. The turning point came after much praying. Harry was in support of my taking the step of faith that I saw as a leap of faith. After I almost made my decision, Harry said, "Sherita, remember that God will not lead you where He won't sustain you." That was my undisputed confirmation to stop work and trust God to provide.

The first few weeks of my not working were tough for me. I had to adjust to being home when the children left for school and day care. Cooking breakfast, getting Harry off to work, having time to clean the house and do laundry during the day were major shifts in my lifestyle. Since answers to prayers are often disguised, I did not see that God was answering my prayer of becoming a real mother to my children.

By having more time during the day, I began to enjoy seeing the children awake before going to my internship assignment. Being able to go to Shari's school for emergencies and just stopping by to see her was refreshing. I began the slow process of spending more time with Shari and Matthew. When I was alone with the children I still was a bit reserved in our interactions. To ease my burden of doing things right, I followed their lead.

From birth, Shari had been a daddy's girl. That fact and knowing that we were both females made the hurdles in our relationship appear higher, but I was determined to do my best to surmount the obstacles. Since Shari always had a strong independent streak, there was no way for me to rush into her life and take over. She would not have allowed me to do so, but eventually we began to bond as mother and daughter. My fear of Shari began to fade to the point where I saw her as a little girl who needed a mother. I continued to listen to Shari's words and body language, and I began to feel a love for her that I did not know was possible between mother and daughter.

I entered Shari's world, meeting her friends and listening to some of her music. The down side was that I wanted to make up for time that was lost in her early years. I soon realized that making up time that had passed was impossible, but I could ask and trust God to restore the years that the "swarming, crawling, consuming, and chewing locust had eaten" (Joel 2:25) while I was too afraid to be a real mom. True to form, as I did what I could do, God provided the increase. I was and am grateful.

After many months I began to feel more comfortable when I was with Shari and Matthew. I gradually moved from being startled by their touch to anticipating their hugs. Emerging from my reservations, I began to initiate giving them hugs and kisses. I began to loosen up and laugh. I accepted the fact that children are not robots but people with opinions that should be heard and issues that should be addressed.

This plan of action was rewarding. Within reason, I was willing to try anything that Shari and Matthew wanted to do. I learned to live with their dirty rooms and their lack of, or limited interest, in things that were important to me. This was a start, a positive start in my becoming a loving mother.

Matthew was and is a person who sees life as a continuous performance. Since he was born during my stage of aloofness, he couldn't really miss the old mommy whom he never knew. Matthew was happy just to entertain me. Shari's close relationship with Harry kept Matthew at bay. Matthew wasn't grasping for more physical space with his daddy, and if he attempted to do so, Shari was not conceding any. I figured out that in order to get close to Matthew, I needed to hug him, smile at him, and watch him. This was simple and difficult for me, but my determination prevailed and all of us reaped the rewards.

The second miracle is that through it all, I've learned to be a mother. By all indications, our children are relatively normal. I enjoy Shari and Matthew. When the mothering finally set in, Harry became jealous of our relationship. But the entire process was in God's time, not mine. As parents we are on an even keel making sure that we are a team in rearing our children.

Shari and Matthew have taken me to another level in life. The thought of losing either one of them terrifies me. I try to let them know every day that I love them. Shari is nearing graduation from high school. Matthew follows four years later. Unless a younger child enters our life, Harry and I will be alone in our home. I pray that I've been the mother that our children needed.

Nurturing taught me that what works for one child does not necessarily apply to another child, even when the children come from the same biological gene pool. Momma often noted the differences in her offspring. Shari and Matthew are two children who express great degrees of love, but they do it in two extremely different ways. Their expressions of love are subject to change without notice.

For years Shari was quiet with her love. After having a story read to her at night, she was ready for a big kiss, a warm hug, and lights out. I watched her as she transitioned to no story, a light kiss, and no hug. From that stage she began to wave her goodbyes and good-nights. Shari never left any doubt about her love for me. Her shy smile, simple questions, and gentle touch said it all.

The most difficult phase with Shari was her change to adolescence when she distanced herself from Harry and me. When she began to chart her personal course as a teenager, she rebelled in a strong way. After many bumps and bruises, Shari realized that her father and I were not her enemies. I thank God for giving me a daughter. She is unique, one-of-a-kind, and I love her.

Matthew loves drama. The more excitement he finds or creates, the better he feels. He says what he thinks. He always has been the hugger and the kisser. He seems more reluctant to change, but when he does change, his phases last longer. He is very difficult to gauge. During a recent outing, Matthew stopped, turned to me, looked me in the eye and said, "Mommy, you have to accept the fact that I'm growing up. I'm not your little baby anymore." Our times of holding hands at the mall and as we cross the street have ended. I miss them, but just as I learned to hold him, I must learn to let go. Matthew was correct: my little baby is growing up. I will survive.

As much as I've tried not to be, as I mother my children, I see my mother in me. The phrase, "Because I'm the momma that's why!" has escaped from my lips. I've been known to utter Momma's phrases of, "Do you think I'm crazy?" and "You expect me to believe *that?*" I've learned that spanking is easy for me and difficult for the children. On the other hand, denying special privileges is much more difficult for all of us. I've learned that I don't know all there is to know about my children and that they have ideas that seem good to them and will be tested by them.

When Momma died, I discovered that nothing and nobody could erase or replace a mother's love. I want my children to know that I always love them, even when they participate in activities that bother me. In examining my evolution into motherhood, I now understand that the fruit of the Spirit, love, has been manifested in a most powerful way. Without the Holy Spirit, a gentleman for a husband, forgiving children, professional help, and caring friends, I would have been lost to the point of no return.

God blessed me with all that I needed to go forth in motherhood. I am grateful.

But someone will say, "You have faith, and I have works." Show me your faith without your works, and I will show you my faith by my works. ... For as the body without the spirit is dead, so faith without works is dead also. —James 2:18, 26

My decision to embrace motherhood was based on faith and works. I could have continued to pray to God, run away from my children, and become a maternal recluse, but I chose to take the risk to become a better mother. Was the result worth the risk? Yes! Would I do it all over again? Yes! In fact, I do it every day. Praise the Lord!

Our children know that they are loved by at least two people, and I am glad to be one of them. Just as Harry's love show-
ered Shari and Matthew earlier, it continues today. Running
away from my children would have caused me to miss a number
of great opportunities for joy and pain, thrills and falls, and love
and trials. No other part of my life has painted such a beautiful
mural of experiences. My feelings have run the gamut from
unlimited highs to devastating lows.

Honestly, I have neither heard nor seen anything that I
would trade for this journey as a mother. I admit, with great
shame, that if Momma had not died I probably would have
missed sharing the genuine mommy experience with my children. Yes, children are a heritage from the Lord. I am blessed that
God chose me to be a nurturer of two members of the heritage.

Mother and Daughter

Since Momma died I have witnessed a vast array of emotions, events, and opportunities. Although each moment has been different from anything I could have imagined, one fact remains constant: the impact of Momma's death will be with me always. I cannot escape this reality.

Except for getting married and the moment when I saw Shari and Matthew for the first time, Momma's dying and death affected me more than any other one-time event in my adult life. A short span of one month and five days left mental and physical images that affect the way I live now. Looking back over the time since Momma died, I realize that my life easily can be divided into two distinct time periods: before Momma died and after Momma died.

What happened to me was clearly complex. Before Momma died I thought that I was unconquerable. I lived as a strong Black woman who had to be in charge of my world and everything in it. This was extremely tiring. I set benchmarks for myself, standards that made me feel worthwhile. Many days were spent wondering how much higher I could raise the bar. For instance, if I did not read at least one book each week, I was a failure. My life was measured by achievements, not so much achievements that other people could see, but achievements that made me feel tall inside.

After Momma died I learned that being strong and vulnerable was not an offense. My strength left room for tears. Being vulnerable helped conquer my fear of people. I remember that when I first went to Benedict, I cried most of the day. My tears were born in the relief of being away from my family of birth; yet I was so afraid of people who weren't in my family. As I grew into womanhood, there were many painful moments where being vulnerable did not pay off for me. But it was during those times of vulnerability that I matured. I learned that not all people are 'bad,' and that those who are described as 'bad' still qualify to be called human beings.

Before Momma died, I was brash with others. This aspect of my attitude allowed me to either hold in my words and feelings altogether or release all of the same with unrelenting stings. Without remorse, I could tell anybody whatever was on my mind. If a person offended me, they probably would know sooner rather than later. When I didn't speak my mind, I was passive-aggressive.

I suppose there were times when people probably didn't know that I had offended them until later. My remarks were not usually openly cold. I chose my words carefully, often using phrases from one of the many books I'd read. I studied people and calculated how they functioned. Were my calculations accurate? Probably not, but that never stopped me from responding to my assessments.

After Momma died, I learned that I didn't have to be nasty to people. The people with whom I came into contact were not a part of my past; they only stood in the shadows of the era. These folks had neither hurt me, nor known my hurt. Why was I so committed to making them pay for what they didn't know and I wasn't willing to say? I began to see that life was not a battle that others fought against me. It was a war that was within me. I chose to strike a peace accord with myself.

God made humans to be in community with one another. In a community setting we learn that we need each other. Before Momma died, I was going solo through life. I was married with children, but I saw life as Harry and his children. I was a separate entity who had never fully relied totally on anyone, including God. From my perspective, I didn't think I needed anyone in my life. I was strong enough and smart enough to accomplish anything I set my heart to do. If my family were present to celebrate with me, so be it, but neither their presence nor approval was a prerequisite for anything I attempted. This was not a deliberate attempt to be estranged. This was the way life had worked best for me all my life. It kept me from being hurt by other people.

Momma's dying and death showed me the value of family and friends. As I listened to friends and relatives talk about how Momma touched their life, I realized that their comments were true and could not have been spoken if Momma had lived her life in the same way I was living mine. By embracing people, Momma embraced a solid life that was filled with many more joys than sorrows. She spent most of her optional time with positive people who probably helped diminish her anguish while helping her enjoy laughter from others and herself.

For the first time in my life, Momma's gregarious lifestyle made good sense to me. The many times that she made us go with her to visit old people, clean people's houses, sit quietly as she took an extra few minutes to listen to somebody tell a story stayed fresh in my mind and heart. Her people skills paid off in a grand way. In sickness and in death people remembered her, and I wanted a piece of that life.

I was not totally antisocial. I could work a crowd and make people feel as if I were okay. My problem: I was a dedicated introvert who was afraid of people. Crowds made me nervous, and people drained me. This was a holdover from childhood where the best days were spent being by myself, while reading, writing, playing my piano, organ, or saxophone, listening to music, and thinking. Since these activities required help from no other human being, I mastered the art of being alone. When Momma died, I caught a glimpse of how the end might be for me. I craved something different.

The faith and works message rose up again. Desiring a different kind of life and working to make a different kind of life went hand in hand. I had no idea how to do what I wanted to do, but I was open for suggestions. I began to study people from a positive standpoint. Harry and Momma had similar personalities. Since Momma was dead, I studied Harry. I noticed how he took time to engage people. He showed a genuine interest in people and what was going on in their world. I began to imitate what I saw, and it worked.

A miracle happened. As I interacted with people, I began to relax with people. The process of changing my ways was not always fun, but it was always interesting. By talking with and listening to people I learned that most people's lives had some kind of mess through which they muddled each day. Stresses and struggles are a part of life, and, in order to survive and retain any degree of sanity, people have to make the necessary adjustments. I learned that I actually am not as much of an outsider as I thought I was.

Before Momma died I had many associates. Other people would call them friends, but for me they were associates. I did have a few friends, some of which came from my being their pastor's wife. Having friends did not fit my definition of a good idea. I did not know how to make friends, and I was not interested in learning the craft. Those who wanted my friendship for reasons that were not beneficial to me had caused much of the pain in my life. To insure my protection from painful interactions, I would steer and stay clear of all personal long-term alliances.

After Momma died I realized that all friendships are not equal. Some friendships require constant companionship while others flourish with distance. I had to determine the different kinds of friendships I wanted, and live accordingly. I took time to do the homework and discovered that I had family friends, ministerial friends, and, yes, even associates. This made the friendship process much easier. In their own way, some people were special to me. This was okay.

There was also the set of genuine friends, people who were my friends because of their relationship with me, not with Harry, the church, or the denomination. With this small circle, I always had the blessing of being comfortable. I could and did find joy in being me. In spending time with these few people, I have learned that I do not have to be afraid of people. I do not have to fit into anyone else's mould, and I must not try to force anyone to fit into mine. Life provides opportunities for everyone, but everyone does not have to be a part of everyone else's world. The choice is mine to make.

I learned how to interact with people in small doses. When the stress started to raise its head, I knew that I had to back off, at least for a while. By being polite, I was able to dismiss myself from gatherings and people, and no love was lost. As time progressed, I became acclimated to being in crowds and being alone with people. I started to accept people for who they said they were until they proved to be somebody else. I learned that others' indiscretions, half-truths, and cover-ups were neither mine, nor of my making. Therefore, I could walk away and be at peace with myself.

My change of lifestyle meant reconstructing my social relationships. Trying to rebuild bridges that I had burned was not easy. As I tried to repair some bridges, strong opposition faced me and refused to yield to my apologies. Others verbally accepted my "I'm sorry," but would not take the chance of trusting me as their friend or associate again. I cannot and will not blame them; I earned the right to be away from them.

To be honest, I decided that some relationships were better left in ruins. Any effort to salvage them would have dug up too much pain and made matters worse than what was needed. I didn't feel comfortable in struggling with certain relationships again, and I decided to move on with my life. Other persons were receptive to me, and, as a result, I continue to communicate with them today.

I am proud to say that as I write this chapter, I do have a few friends. They differ in age and race, but they are my true friends. These are the people who tell me when I'm wrong, and they do so in love. I am allowed to bounce my weird ideas off these people; yet they don't tell me that I'm insane. I believe that all parts of the reconciliation process have worked to my good and God's glory.

When I was going through the rough times in my relationship with Harry and my mental self, my friends were there for me, but they stayed away from the fray. Although I gave them the silent treatment on my personal life, they knew something was seriously wrong. Still, they didn't pry, attack me, or judge me. They prayed for me to be strong enough to overcome the struggle.

One of my friends, a minister's wife, keeps me on my toes as far as being supportive of Harry's ministry. A group of A.M.E. women preachers are always there for me. Another friend gives me ministerial support from a non-A.M.E. perspective; we think alike, but she is much more peacefully radical than I. We complement each other. One friend and I have known each other since I was four years old and she was three; this is probably the only friendship that has never wavered. I have a few friends from my college days at Benedict. And then there's my newest friend, an older person of a different race and culture. It is with her that I can share my thoughts on racial differences, reconciliation, and social justice. And, yes, I confess that I do have friends at Union Bethel.

Concerning my siblings, we have a good relationship. I try to stay in touch with each of them regularly. Surviving Momma's death has been and is difficult for us. Each of us deals with our loss in the best manner that we know. Sometimes we talk about Momma and laugh. There have been times when we have cried. But most of the time we are silent about our being motherless.

We all wish that Momma were still alive. I believe that it is humanly impossible to fully explain how a parent's death affects the children. The good and bad times merge together, sometimes blurred by tears and traced by the same, to form streaks of sorrow and hope in our lives. We didn't lose our mother; she died. But for good or for ill, her legacy is alive, not only in us, but also in all whose lives she touched.

There was a time in my life when I wanted to kill myself. I was convinced that I had nobody that I could call as a friend or trust to come to my aid. Now that I've learned that life is worth living, I am able to celebrate life in its fullest. I still am an introvert. Large crowds still make me nervous, but I know that I can survive in crowds. I know that I can only try to control myself, and, at times, that task provides a tedious struggle.

I still miss Momma. Some days I feel as if she died just yesterday. Momma and I didn't see eye-to-eye on many things, but, now that I have Shari, I know that our strains were present because she was my mother and I was her daughter. As I think about Momma's teachings, I understand her motives better. She wanted the best for me. She knew that my best was different from my siblings' best.

I, like Momma, get excited about seeing people display good manners. "Please," "Thank you," and "Excuse me" were constant phrases in Momma's vocabulary that have been grafted into mine. I don't think that either of us ever regretted using those words. For it has been in those words that new relationships have been birthed and nurtured.

When I pass away from this life to the next and all is said about me and done with me, I want to have the same kind of peace that Momma exhibited. I want to know that somebody cared enough about me to permit me to be a part of their life. When I die I want to be missed because of good works and kind deeds to others. I see now, more than ever, that as I have come into my own as a wife, mother, sister, and friend, I am very much like my mother. What a blessing!

The book of James serves as an encouragement to my faith.

...count it all joy when you fall into various trials, knowing that the testing of your faith produces patience. But let patience have its

perfect work, that you may be perfect and complete, lacking noth-
ing. —James 1:2-4

These verses continue to provide the support I need as I continue to adjust to Momma's death. Yes, I still have questions. No, I don't believe that God will provide acceptable answers for all that I want to know. However I trust that Momma's death has made me a stronger Christian. I can say that although I miss Momma, I count her as a very special angel who was assigned to me.

When Momma died, and the pain of her death set in, I thought my life was over. I had no joy. Everything in my world changed for the worst. As I read the passage in James now, I understand that I could not have survived the ordeal of Momma's death without having faith in God. When I couldn't pray and didn't want to seek God for anything that had to do with Momma's death, God was working for my good.

My faith was tested by my mother's death. But now I rejoice! God used this traumatic period in my life to make me stronger. Being in a situation where I could do nothing to change either what had happened or what was happening, I had to trust God, and only God, to bring me through the storm. My Christian character began to leave the womb to try surviving in a harsh environment that is known to many people as life. Because of this trial, I am a better person.

After more than nine years since Momma's death, I see her leaving this earth, her family, and me as a blessing in disguise. By taking away my maternal crutch, God has blessed me to stand up and grow spiritually. I am convinced that Momma's death has made me stronger in every aspect of my life. The ministry to which God has called me is better because I have learned to trust in God.

I still miss Momma. I wish she were here with all of us, her family, especially her grandchildren. Hardly a day goes by that I don't think of her in some way. As I mature in marriage, mothering, and ministry, there are many things I'd like to share with her. And I do. In my own way, I tell her what's happening. I ask her how she would handle particular situations. Of course she doesn't provide an audible response, but somehow Momma gets her message across. This is accomplished by my reflecting on how she lived and how, in so doing, she taught me to do the same.

Thanks, Momma!

About the Author

The Reverend Sherita Moon Seawright was born and raised in Clinton, South Carolina. She received her elementary and high school education at the public schools in Cross Hill and Clinton, South Carolina.

In 1979 she received a Bachelor of Arts in Political Science, *summa cum laude* at Benedict College in Columbia, South Carolina. In 1980 she received a Master of Arts, Political Science from the Ohio State University in Columbus, Ohio. She went on to receive a Master of Divinity from Howard University School of Divinity, Washington, DC in 1993.

Other accomplishments are as follows:

• Daniel Foundation Scholarship at Benedict
• Strom Thurmond Scholarship at Benedict
• Minority Master's Fellowship at Ohio State
• Ford Foundation Fellowship at Howard
• Benjamin E. Mays Fellowship at Howard
• 1993 Dean's Award for Academic Excellence, Howard University
• Congress of National Black Churches Fellow (1992-1993)
• Itinerant Elder, African Methodist Eiscopal (A.M.E.) Church
• A facilitatior at the 18th Episcopal District's (A.M.E. Church) HIV/AIDS Conference in Botswana, Southern Africa
• Assistant Pastor, Union Bethel AME Church in Brandywind, Maryland
• Executive Director, Bethel House, Inc., Brandywine, Maryland

She is the wife of the Reverend Dr. Harry L. Seawright and the mother of two children, Shari Nicole and Harry Matthew.

When Momma Died—A Journey to Self
Order Form

Postal orders: Sherita M. Seawright
Post Office Box 44527
Fort Washington, MD 20744

Telephone orders: (301) 265-1816

Please send *When Momma Died—A Journey to Self* **to:**

Name: _____

Address: _____

City: _____ State: _____

Zip: _____

Telephone: (_____) _____

Total Number of Copies Ordered: _____

Book Price: $15.00

Shipping: $3.00 for the first book and $1.00 for each additional book
to cover shipping and handling within US, Canada, and
Mexico. International orders add $6.00 for the first book
and $2.00 for each additional book

Or order from:
ACW Press
5501 N. 7th. Ave. #502
Phoenix, AZ 85013

(800) 931-BOOK

or contact your local bookstore